*What people are saying about **Embodying Spirit**…*

Jacquelyn Small pushes ahead the frontiers of self-understanding. Full of wisdom and insight, *Embodying Spirit* is a most valuable tool for our personal inner journey.
> —**Peter Russell**, author of *The White Hole in Time*
> and *The Global Brain*

A book written with verve—charms the heart and mind into birthing an active creativity. Jacquelyn Small shows us how to make meaning work for us.
> —**June Singer**, author of *Boundaries of the Soul*

Jacquelyn Small is one of the few who dares to offer a vision of hope for our times. Her combination of spirituality and psychological insights aid us in imagining the mature human.
> —**Robert Moore, Ph.D.**, co-author of *The Magician Within*

A mind and heart-expanding adventure in consciousness by a passionate and wise guide. In *Embodying Spirit*, Jacquelyn Small brings her fire and insight to creatively illumine the duality of our psychological and spiritual selves.
> —**Robert and Judith Gass**, creators of
> "The Opening the Heart" workshops

Jacquelyn Small effortlessly brings together the mysticism of the East with the psychologically based healing modalities of the West. *Embodying Spirit* is an expression of meditation-in-motion, an effortless flow of wisdom, insight, and knowledge.
> —**Yogi Amrit Desai**, founder and spiritual director
> of Kripalu Yoga Center

I believe that Jacquelyn Small's psychological work is some of the most important work being done anywhere. She is truly a planetary worker. With *Embodying Spirit*, she gives us a prescription for living with greater spontaneity and the freedom to "fly" beyond the banal.
> —**Jeremiah Abrams**, author of *The Shadow In America*

EMBODYING SPIRIT

EMBODYING SPIRIT

Coming Alive with Meaning and Purpose

JACQUELYN SMALL

HAZELDEN®

Hazelden Education Materials
Center City, Minnesota 55012-0176

© 1994 by Jacquelyn Small
All rights reserved. Published 1994
Printed in the United States of America
No portion of this publication may be
reproduced in any manner without the
written permission of the publisher

Library of Congress Cataloging-in-Publication Data
Small, Jacquelyn.
    Embodying spirit : coming alive with meaning and purpose /
Jacquelyn Small.
        p.   cm.
    Includes bibliographical references and index.
    ISBN: 0-89486-994-9
    1. Dualism.   2. Good and evil.   3. Mind and body.   4.Ego
(Psychology)   I. Title.
B812.S63   1994
128—dc20   94-29840
                                                           CIP

Editor's note
    Hazelden Educational Materials offers a variety of information
on chemical dependency and related areas. Our publications do
not necessarily represent Hazelden's programs, nor do they offi-
cially speak for any Twelve Step organization.

This book is dedicated to The Beloved.

And to those of you who, like me, fly close to the sun…
sometimes burning your wings! And to others of you
who, like me, get bogged down in your conditions, feeling
"wingless," forgetting that you can fly. You are my
inspiration for this book, my fellow travelers.
I love you all!

CONTENTS

Our Insatiable Craving to Be Both Human and Divine *16*; The Cry for Transcendence *24*.

The Law of Antinomy: A New Dispensation for the Third Millennium *25*; "The Evolutionary Mystic": The Blend of Science and Spirituality *29*; The Symbolic Level of Reality: Coming Alive with Meaning and Purpose! *32*; Complexes Are Symbolic/Archetypal, Too *35*.

The Opposites Within Are Lovers *41*; An Ever-Expanding View of God *42*; The Paradigm Shift in a Nutshell *46*; The Purpose of the Open Heart *48*.

In Appreciation

To Judy Delaney, my editor at Hazelden, for her mastery in hearing my "voice" and luring my kaleidoscopic brain into a format that enhances my writings so magically. I am in awe of her abilities, and I have cherished our times of deep sharing and commitment to this project.... Only a beginning for us.

To Tom Grady, Barbara Moulton, and Robin Seaman of HarperSanFrancisco, for their tremendous support and accessibility in the production of this book. Thank you all for holding such a sacred space for my inspirations. And to Sue Rolfe for her caring liaison work.

To Greg Zelonka, my business partner, for his loyal support in keeping Eupsychia's work going while I disappear into my computer for months to write books such as this.

To Jacquie Thomas and Brenda Shea of Eupsychia, for their daily support, integrity, and encouragement that helps me unfold "the dream."

To the teaching consultants, staff, and dear friends of Eupsychia who, through their inspired therapeutic abilities, clear and compassionate support, and psychospiritual being, bring alive the concepts and experiential work for which Eupsychia stands—Sue Jane White, Karen Yuskaitis, Jim Frazier, Catherine Penn, Jennifer DeLoach, Linda Piscitelli, Robert Yuskaitis, Greta Stromberg, Rob Buntz, Greg Stephens, Karen Zelonka, Robby Piscitelli, Don Wegscheider, Jeannine Farr-Edelman, Joel Edelman, Kitty

Farmer, Byron Metcalf, Diane Magliolo, Frances Cox, Nancy Dorsett, Connie Dominy, Bill Green, Kay Christopher, June and Bronek Zelonka, Curtis Byford, Philip Sansone, Tom Bullard, Michael Keene, Donna Crews, and all the volunteers.

To the students/teachers who come through Eupsychia's process for training in Psychospiritual Integration. Without you, this work could never have taken form, for you are the work.

And to my loving "extended family" who have been there for me and for my son, Brett, during our trying times with my parents' deaths and Brett's illness—my heart is full of gratitude for your warm support and physical presence— Nancy Somers, Mark Blumenthal, Jerry Cunningham, Tom and Michele Gee, Carol Macey, and the entire Towery clan. Without your sustenance and heart's love, this book could have never gone to press.

I am deeply grateful to you all for helping me with "my part" and for having such a deep reverence for this ongoing living process.

A SPECIAL THANKS

I want to honor a special group of outstanding public speakers, teachers, and presenters with whom Eupsychia has collaborated for our "Embodying Spirit" conferences and other events we've held throughout North America in the area of personal and planetary transformation:

Jeremiah Abrams

Emile Conrad Da'oud

Ram Dass

Amrit Desai (Gurudev)

Larry Dossey

Dunya

Matthew Fox

Robert and Judith Gass

Shakti Gawain

Stanislav and Christina Grof

Joan Halifax

Barbara Hamilton

Kathleen and Gay Hendricks

Jean Houston

Barbara Marx Hubbard

Sam Keen

Michael Mayer

Robert Moore

Thomas Moore

Gabrielle Roth

Ilana Rubenfeld
Peter Russell
June Singer
Malidoma Somé and his wife, Sobonfu
Patricia Sun
Robert Wilkinson
Fred Alan Wolf
Marion Woodman
Gary Zukav

As "voices on the threshold of our future," you each embody a deep sense of knowing that we are part of a greater Plan. I honor each of you for your unique contribution to this amazing ascension in consciousness in which we are all so intensely involved, for the fertile "seeds" you are sowing in our minds that are helping us link back to our Source. Thank you for your willingness to step out from beyond our paradigm-bound thinking to courageously remind us of our souls' original purpose and larger life.

How To Use This Book—
The Kaleidoscope of Consciousness

New-paradigm thinking, on which this material is based, functions more like a kaleidoscope than a linear progression; it grabs you while you're looking the other way. If you are one of those people who is basically left-brained and likes to study in an orderly fashion, this book might be a frustrating experience. So I want to say this right up front: though this writing respects a linear/analytical mind, it also honors the creatively chaotic; its structure may confront you with contradiction. You won't find completed recipes here, nor a well-defined "new psychology" or perfect "healing plan." This would be an insult to your creative intelligence! Your intuition picks up ideas differently from the way your intellect does. But these seemingly opposite modes of listening and learning should not rub and jostle each other in the slightest as you read, for they interact harmoniously on the *inner* side of life.

This book is meant to incite your creativity, to inspire and validate you for what you already know. Each of you has your own sphere of influence, far beyond this author's understanding. If you are open to what is presented here, "feeling" your way into it, flashes of recognition, revelations, and inspired hunches will lead to your own ways of using it. You may open the book to any page and perhaps you'll find something that lights the fire of recognition (re-cognition). This is how your soul "remembers." Creative ideas may occur to you as you draw on your own experiences and synthesize this your way. I believe with all my heart that from the pages that follow, you will build on your own knowledge and expertise by creatively using both your left- and right-brain skills.

You'll discover that this book is layered with several levels of information. Some of it will speak to you exactly where you are now in your life, while other parts may seem to pass by you. So please, take from these pages only what fits for you. If any of these words call forth a moment of insight or inspiration for you, then let those words be heard. But not otherwise!

I hope you find this work inspiring and that the messages and insights will prod your own "future memory" and ease your transition through these challenging times of rapid change.

Note: The quotes in boldface print throughout this book are inspired messages I received from my inner Beloved, the soul.

PROLOGUE:
ARISING FROM SLUMBER

When the ego looks out and sees that it's running to the edge of its own demise, a little bell goes off, and a call goes out....

In 1975, on August 13, the day before my birthday, I had a waking dream. By this, I mean I was awake and sleeping at the same time. My waking and dream states had merged. This dream was what I call A Big Dream, for it changed my life. I recorded it in my journal, thank God! So I can share it now with you:

We make our beds, and we lie in them.
We go to sleep, and then we dream....

In my dream, I was lying sleepily in my bed, saying this to myself like a chant.

In my outer life, I was still dreamily and innocently enchanted by mass consciousness. Hypnotized. I was busily absorbing humanity's conditions. And not even questioning anything; just "doing" like everyone else. You may be sleepily coming out of this state right now. The dream continued:

Quite suddenly, from somewhere deep inside,
As I lay there on my bed,
I heard the sound of a Call;

I even saw a vision of the Caller.
He appeared to me in a flash
in vivid technicolor;
I could see him from the waist up.
Shocked at seeing this great Being,
I began to stir....

As I lay there on my bed, half asleep and half awake, a vague and distant but familiar "future memory" made me restless, reminding me of something I was to do, something that felt quite urgent.... I could even hear that Voice plainly now, inside my head, and I knew Him as that One who had kept me company as a child. In my dream,

I sat up and looked around. And then I stared
in utter amazement at what unfolded
before my eyes.
Where am I? And what time is it?
I cried out in my dream.
And I almost panicked!
I saw that we've all been oversleeping.
And that it's getting very late!

In the dream, I stood up and looked around and began to reflect sadly upon the mess we've made of our world. I was still groggy, puzzled, and confused. I saw that my familiar life had become stale, too familiar. It could no longer gratify me in the same old all-too-human ways. I saw us about to get on the move. We are all starving. We've been busily feeding our egos, but as spiritual beings, it's spiritual food we crave! Being a religious person, I knew that God had to be in this somewhere.

Still not fully aware of all the implications of what was about to occur, I realized there are others out there who are feeling this same yearning and discontent, others just as hungry as I am who've also gobbled up all the nutrients in their feeding ground....

In my dream, I cried out:

Who created this scenario in the first place?
And what am I doing here?

And the answer came once more, from the Voice inside my head:

You did, my dear ones. Don't you recall?
Separately and together, and through your
own design—
but with My input, of course.
Perhaps I must remind you that
You are a part of Me.
Though you do not remember quite yet,
You are made in my image.

I seemed to fall into a state of reverie for a moment or two. And a vague feeling of familiarity slowly crept over me, and time seemed to disappear. Then, as though a "future memory" came clear, I felt myself imbedded in the human condition, and not "just human" at all. I saw that we've been seeing it all backwards, like a mirrored reflection, looking in the wrong direction. Like Narcissus, who had been hypnotically staring at his own reflection, I stood up now and looked out into the Real World. And everything was clear. I knew who I was once more, and bliss poured through me. I looked out through the eyes of my spiritual Self, and saw quite plainly that we've done this for the love of God.

While still in the dream

**I tidied up my bed
and stepped out into my fragile new world.
I was feeling very different
from how I'd ever felt before.**

And it began to fade.

I jumped up and ran to my mirror to see if I could see my reflection! And there I was, staring back at myself, in all my glory! I was awake!

Though I did not realize this until many years later, my Journey had begun....

From this new vantage point, the preoccupation with my past and outer world of frantic activity began to fade slowly. I was aware of another directive force—a new gravity field— pulling me in fast-forward movement. The attraction was so strong, I could do nothing but follow it. And so my story goes.

My hunger pangs are increasing now, as I sense what is to come—not just for me, but for us all. Even though I really haven't a clue about what's coming, or even where we'll all be next year, I know that I will follow along, for I see now that

**It is our Future who beckons.
Our destiny is on the move,
inviting us to consciously take part.
Of course, I am willing! I thought,**

**for as a grown up and restless Daughter of God,
what else is there to do?"**

The truth of our nature now stands revealed before my inner eye. And I'm beginning to settle down, with a strong conviction that it's all okay. To help keep me awake, on the mirror in my room I've placed this message from an inner Guide, the Tibetan master Dwhal Khul, for it comforts me and helps hold me steady anytime the going gets rough. Perhaps, during your darker times, it will console you, too:

Nothing under heaven can arrest the progress of the human soul on its pilgrimage from darkness to light, from the unreal to the real, and from death to immortality.

I tell you this story of my dream of awakening, so you can more easily recognize your own bigger life unfolding from within. For our time of completion has come, dear brothers and sisters of my soul. Of this, I am quite certain. Humanity is experiencing a "destiny transfer." And we are all heading Home.

INTRODUCTION

The soul once turned toward matter, fell in love with it, and, burning with desire to experience bodily pleasures, was no longer willing to tear herself away from it. And so the world was born.
—*Daniel Chwolsohn,* Die Ssabier und der Ssabismus

As human beings we were inherently designed to merge the "angel" and the "fallen angel" within, the primordial conflict that has plagued us since the beginning of Time. It is human nature to crave the experience of fading back into the comforting wholeness of eternal, undifferentiated Bliss.

Paradoxically, it is also human nature to separate from others and seek our own creative expression. The *ego* differentiates us; it is the aspect of us concerned with building something special to be noticed and rewarded by the societal world. And as we must each develop "one small measure" of the God expression, the Soul individuates in each of us and urges us toward the one Self of which we are all a part. When we explore the meaning of the words *individuate* and *differentiate*, we are provided with a clue to the paradox: To individuate means to form an indivisible whole, an undivided entity! To differentiate means to stand out as different. Some aspects of life serve to unite us, while others divide. And both types of experience seem necessary for our advancement. To get beyond this duality of the ego and the soul—to avoid feeling pulled apart by these opposing drives—we can learn to be in both places at once: unified *and* unique.

9

This book is meant to stir your soul. It speaks of a spiritual psychology for reclaiming your whole nature. Our ego-nature has come to the edge of this world it has so cleverly invented. And no one knows this better than the ego itself, for it's feeling quite discontented these days! The ego side of our nature served us well in bringing us to where we are now: We've become masters of the material ways of our ego-dominated world. But now, it has run out of ways to move us past our discontent.

When the soul awakens in the world of the ego, a little bell goes off inside us and we start to crave a higher purpose. We begin looking intuitively for a way to lift out of our old patterns. Often we do not realize this process consciously—at least, not at first. It is the intuition and not the logic that recognizes the call. This "sacred hunger" we start to feel is the urge for transcendence. At times such as these, our greater Self walks into our consciousness and overtakes the ego's limited ways. This greater Self is our true identity, and its purpose is to bring us into a higher and more integrated state of being. This higher, transpersonal Self is the archetype that will carry us forward into our new expression. And it already exists within us, for it is the root-consciousness, the core from which we all emerged. Our blueprint for wholeness, the divine Self, is present within the psyche. It is our Divine Core.

However! There is a snag in this holy Scheme (as there is in any divine endeavor); the Self must become embodied. The Self is of a "hybrid" species, being made of both spirit and earthly substance. And these opposing aspects of the Self are meant to live in harmony.

To incarnate here, the divine archetypal Self must somehow create a sacred union of the ego and the soul. And then this Self can be conceived, welcomed here as real. This process is the embodiment of spirit. This divine union of the ego and soul, and the ordeals we must face for their eventual sacred union, is humanity's current evolutionary task. We will all take this Journey of Love at some point, if we're to become whole. And as with all Journeys of Love, it can be a life-threatening adventure. Seeking to unite two so contradictory natures as the ego and the soul brings all the paradoxes of love and hate, of both heaven and hell. Apparently, there's no way around this, for through this very struggle of "divine tension" of our two opposing natures, the higher Self is born. And we thought we had to be *either* human *or* divine, loving one, while fearing or hating the other.

If we're carefully prepared and follow the rules of the road (for true mystics have always known of this path), this tension between the two ways of being can become a place of great promise. We will be presented with new possibilities to satisfy our innate hunger as a hybrid species, to be both human and divine. But travelers must be prepared, for we are required to undergo great ordeals that hone the capacities this new way demands: We'll be challenged over and over to stay open-minded and flexible and to heed the road signs that point the way.

Our hardest task will be to dissolve the crippling dualism trapping us, where we thought we were only human or only divine. We will need to do what seems impossible: to walk paradoxically in two worlds at once, inhabiting an earthly body with spiritual intent. With hearts open and minds keen, we'll live in and interpret both worlds at once through our ordinary daily routines. In practical ways, our ego and soul learn to commune and combine creatively, and respect each other's role in this sacred work of embodying Spirit. From the inside out we'll be shown how to *be* this new synthesis of ego and soul. Then, as dedicated spiritual beings in human form, we'll be doing "our part" in the co-creation and embodiment of a brand new world. Some call this "manifesting heaven on earth." And this is our evolutionary task as mediators of the human world and the divine. This Great Work has been known throughout the Ages as the "path of direct knowing," which can only be learned one way—through our living experience.

"Divine tension" accompanies our work in this world when we are aligned with this Higher Self. We'll often identify with Rabia's plight in this Sufi song, for people who've traveled the spiritual path of direct experience:

> *"Rabia, Rabia, why are you weeping?"*
> *the people asked, and Rabia replied:*
> *"I am sorrowing," she said.*
> *"But Rabia, Rabia, why are you sorrowing?"*
> *the people asked, and Rabia replied:*
> *"I am eating the bread of this world*
> *While doing the work of that world."*
>
> *—Zuleika*

Like Rabia, we'll find a poignant sadness to this state of being as we look around and see many of the messes we've made, and all we're leaving behind. We're greatly attached to some of our old ways; they've become familiar and safe. And we've been mostly ignorant of the harm we've created here, for we've all been asleep.

Yet it also feels like the bliss of anticipated love, to be moving ahead toward a great unknown. There is an inner exhilaration that compels us onward. With our eyes wide open, we can see all the suffering humanity created here. We can no longer deny our responsibilities as conscious co-creators of something better. Now we must surrender to a Higher Power, and trust that our divine Guidance will come.

Chapter One

"DIVINE DISCONTENT"

If you bring forth what is within you, what you bring forth will save you. If you do not bring forth what is within you, what you do not bring forth will destroy you.

—*The Gospel of St. Thomas: Logion 45*

The most important tool we have for the process of Self-creation is the controversial quality of our Desire. Throughout history there has raged a battle between East and West, wherein one views "desirelessness" as the highest good, while the other appears caught in a frantic search for gratification. When we attempt to resolve this dualism with spiritual dogma, we fall short of resolution. On the one hand, living without desire doesn't seem authentic. On the other, it seems our desires are evil and catapult us uncontrollably toward personal disaster.

Dr. Carl Gustav Jung provided a way to synthesize this apparent paradox by defining desire as a "combination of pleasure and the urge to individuate." With this definition, desire translates into a commitment to the experience of the forces of life as it is, a path of consciously commited action. Dr. Jung warned that if we attempt to give up desire prematurely, we can become "psychic corpses" and perish from "psychic pernicious anemia," lacking the motivation necessary to individuate. We can view the descent into the Earth's raw, transformative forces of vitality and tribulation as the link with Heaven's mission for us. I hope you will feel a sense of relief as you hear this validation of your human passions as having a sacred function.

OUR INSATIABLE CRAVING TO BE BOTH HUMAN AND DIVINE

Seeking "the delights of the flesh" has ancient roots within the human design. And so do feelings of guilt and wrong for wanting such pleasures. Our ordinary human desires are often thought of as "selfish." We've been taught it is sinful to have passionate human desires, especially sexual feelings. Some forms of religion, in fact, are so restrictive and judgmental, members must hide most of their human feelings and urges, wearing plastic smiles on their faces, needing to appear above and beyond such "lower needs." You may recall a humorous country-and-western song that goes: "You've gotten so heavenly, you ain't no earthly good."

So here is the other side of the story, for we can't win in this incessant battle between good and evil. Not as long as misguided or half-alive human beings are in charge of our morality! There is a term we use in our work that describes people who try to be only "heavenly," or *always* positive and loving. We say they are in a *spiritual bypass*—a phrase coined by psychologist John Welwood—for people who are this lopsided can never truly be themselves. And we don't trust them, because we never know what is really going on behind the sunny facades.

Either way we view our nature, whether looking up or down, we tend to separate our earthly self from our spiritual self, as though one is bad, the other good. Our inability to understand the troublesome conflicts within us has led many an unsteady soul into the lure of addiction or neurosis—a treacherous road that no one would ever *consciously* choose. It is completely natural to love both the sensuous pleasures and the feelings of being holy and high. Yet these either lusty or lofty pursuits tend to split apart within our psyche. If they are not integrated, they can get us into a great deal of trouble.

We've all been taught since we were very young that nations divided within cannot be strong. This is true of the human psyche as well. To be split off from any part of our natural instincts and urges—the traits that are most "species-like," the traits that give us our very definition as earthlings—can be crazy-making. If we cannot integrate and make conscious all parts of ourselves, our denied parts have no place to go but into the closets of repression, deep in our subconscious. They are still present nonetheless, and eventually our feelings will pop out unexpectedly, now exaggerated, and they'll usually embarrass or disgrace us in some awful manner. This explains how an especially rigid, righteous person can proselytize against "sins of the flesh," and also have a dark and lurid "secret life"! Sadly for us humans, we've lost what the ancient Greek Orthodox Church knew:

This very power of desire within your souls imprints the nature of God—which is Love—upon your lives. (Capsanis 1992)

There is a natural impetus in human nature that moves us toward the sanctification of our desires, for we are always hungry to merge with the divine. And this urge is so strong because we are so human!

It is through this constant "divine discontent," this feeling of always seeking a greater identity, that you will eventually evolve into a replica of your Ideal.

I am awed by the truth of this statement as it comes onto my computer! It's hard to understand how we got so far out of touch with our compelling and vibrant nature. And then, to define it as bad. To passionately "live in God and let God live in us," (Capsanis 1992) then, is our highest goal. For in this way, God's nature of Love and Desire moves toward us, and is absorbed by us. And since we are made in His image, we actually become this desire and love our own divinity as well as our humanness—we "take on God-nature."

The bottom line for most of us is this: During those times we are moving in a forward and higher direction, we are quite pleased with ourselves. Life seems worth living, even during the worst times. In fact, *often* during the hard times—for during times of personal crisis, our energies become intense and imbued with meaning. When we experience this "high," we are living in God and God is living in us. We are for that time, at least, in ecstasy. We find a deep meaning and purpose to this existence, almost the erotic gratification that accompanies any fulfilling affair of the heart. And if we somehow lose it, our ecstasy turns into the agony of despair.

Religious agony/ecstasy has been evident throughout the ages and was deeply honored in the early Christian church. The ancient Greek Orthodox Church, for instance, believed that God looks out through our eyes. In ancient times, humans were seen as divine. And for these early Christians, learning to embody variations on the theme of Life and Love was the equivalent of doing God's will. It is possible that even through the Christian religious life, we were never intended to externalize some "Old Man in the Sky" as our ultimate authority, but instead, we were meant to act creatively and morally under our own steam. In fact, morality to these early Christians was the alignment of a philosophy of life with rapturous living. This made for good-ness in human nature.

But always, ecstatic extremes have been feared because they put us in a high energy state too exotic to contain. Today, in fact, we seem to have lost this sanctification of our human desires almost completely, seeing them as immoral. We run from what we truly crave to avoid becoming obsessed. Perhaps we are afraid we might find that, once experienced, we could not live without it.

Perhaps here lies the real cause of our neurotic pain and all the disorderly addictions that carry us to the extremes of our passionate nature: We are afraid to claim what gives us the most pleasure in life and go for it. Instead, we seek sub-stitutes for God. And still we do not find fulfillment.

You might find it interesting to stop right now and reflect on what it is you truly want, in your deepest heart of hearts, and see if you are moving toward it. Or is it only a dream that, in resignation and disbelief, you've decided will never come true.

We both fear and adore our passions and the delicious fruits of this earthly existence. This sensual/emotional feeling level of life is where many people experience the deepest splits, imbalances, and confusions. All these unintegrated desires and misunderstandings keep us divided within. Ultimately they keep us from becoming unified with the Inner Beloved, our Divine Self. For we dare not dream that a True Love so wonderful could live right inside our own skin.

Our cravings bring us face to face with the human shadow, those still unconscious parts of ourselves we deplore and disown. Learning ways to heal these unwanted parts is more than half the work of embodying spirit, our *psychospiritual integration*. To heal, we must return to our past and literally "re-collect" all these lost pieces of ourselves. This process of purification and acceptance of our disowned nature is a prerequisite for any spiritual transformation. There is a time-worn maxim in spiritual work: You can't move to a higher level until you accept fully where you're at.

Our alienation from our deeper Self, with the companion feelings of isolation and shame must be fully experienced before they can be transformed. "Not out, but through!" becomes the psyche's cry as it learns it must experience its own dramatic bout with darkness, the negative side of its nature, before it can complete itself.

Why? Because if we only pursue the light, we deny the shadow of our own nature and project it on others. Hatred, bigotry, even war have their psychodynamic roots in this phenomenon of projection. The negativity within us, being only one side of our nature, holds its power only by remaining in the dark. Once accepted, the compulsion to act from these incompleted dark elements within us subsides, and they are balanced by the positive qualities of their opposites. We reclaim and accept our whole nature.

There is a correlation between the shadow's ways, feelings of ecstasy, and our addictive nature, for each operates in the closets of fear and repression—the inability to own the passionate and "untamed" side of our nature. But as you read, you'll start to see that even the lowliest shadow self has a purposeful and holy function: that somehow, having to hit bottom is a sacred ritual, an integral part of the creative process. Our passions are obviously tied to the act of creation itself. And who would know more about the activities of creation than the Creator-God who invented them?

I hope you now have a sense of the "holy conflict" within our desire nature, but that you also realize that all can eventually be resolved into a life filled with divine ecstasy and love. Apparently, the Higher Power has plans for our path to heaven other than letting us simply choose between the opposites of right or wrong, moral or immoral, passionate or blasé. Transcendence is a battle between "the warring opposites," which then both rise to a higher way. These are the workings of creativity itself.

Most of us feel we're a long way from harmonizing our holy and unholy aspects. We prefer to project our despicable shadow self onto others and denounce it from a distance, a peculiar psychological defense mechanism we'll speak of later. This acceptance of our whole nature requires a shift in consciousness we can't take for granted. We may need to do a great deal of inner work before we can resolve these splits which tear many an unconscious soul apart.

A reframing of our biographies and a new identity may be in order if we're ever going to get past this uncomfortable stage of our human unfoldment. The work needed will be that of psychospiritual integration. As natural transcenders, we must learn to accept ourselves as the lucky possessors of insatiable appetites, hungry hearts, and minds that are starving for truth. For without this craving, we would fall into a state of entropy and never push forward. The craving, the hunt, the heady anticipation of "the seeker," of going toward some deep and unmet yearning, always seeking a greater high—perhaps this is the true blessing of being alive! And even more: perhaps it's God's way of keeping us on a path of transcendence. It could be that this is why our Future continually beckons but never really arrives. Our "divine discontent" assures us that we'll never rest in any sort of incompletion—again and again we feel capable of going beyond our current state. Perhaps this is how we eventually simulate our God-nature and merge with our Ideal.

You might be confused about this urge to go higher, believing you are supposed to give up your passions and be "spiritual." But transcendence isn't leaving life; it is living life more abundantly, more expressive of your rich potential! Mythologist Joseph Campbell said that trancendence is learning to "follow our bliss" with wholehearted participation in the rapture of being alive. When we begin to suffocate in our polluted environment and stale beliefs, we intuitively seek spiritual sustenance, love, commitment to a higher purpose. We need these reminders to transcend our unfulfilling, dualistic ways.

And when we try to rise above something we've not fully accepted and integrated, the very Law of Transcendence itself will bring us right back, as though to say: "Stay put until you get it right! This current task is your highest pleasure."

The Law of Transcendence does not command you to leave life, to simply rise above it; it prompts you to live your life more abundantly, more expressive of your full potential. This has always been misunderstood. Transcendence is easily misunderstood.

Carl Jung warns that we humans have a strange and paradoxical resistance to knowing fully who we are. So from the very start, it seems we must embrace this inherent conflicting nature of ours: both the one who remains unattached and above it all, and the one who enters and takes the ride:

The only thing that really matters now is whether man can climb up to a...higher plane of consciousness.... Unfortunately, a terrifying ignorance prevails in this respect, and an equally great aversion to increasing the knowledge of his intrinsic nature. (Jung, 1973: para. 746)

THE CRY FOR TRANSCENDENCE

Now, because of splits within our nature, we are people in desperation, searching for a new vision and hoping for a future we can believe in. Yet this new life will not be found outside us anywhere. We must resolve our seemingly endless search for the passionate and sacred from within ourselves, being reborn in Truth through an opening in the collective unconscious mind. Only in the vastness of the psyche's larger life are ideals spawned and does creativity flourish in unimagined potential. As co-creators we are restless now, wanting to find a new feeding ground and make a way of life that befits our deeper urges. We are starving for the kind of food that nourishes both our human and spiritual nature; therefore, though many of us would like to,

We cannot just go out and save the world; we must first save the psyche who images the world!

Chapter Two

THE PARADIGM SHIFT: WHAT IS IT?

When you believe it, you'll see it.
—Wayne Dyer

THE LAW OF ANTINOMY:
A NEW DISPENSATION FOR THE THIRD MILLENNIUM

Evolution brings us new cosmic laws that we need to understand to be in step with the greater scheme of things. The Law of Antinomy is such a law, newly explicated by Dr. Carl Jung. This law says: At the deepest level of our nature, two complementary opposites reside harmoniously within the whole—a totality of opposites. The Chinese yin/yang symbol expresses this universal law. This principle dissolves all duality, from the highest to the lowest manifestation, reminding us that we are *both* human *and* divine, and never either/or. This law, in fact, reminds us that *all* opposites within us are always two sides of the same thing. Currently Humanity is passing through an open door into a new dimension of consciousness, one where we will all realize our Immortality—spiritual beings in human bodies.

But "immortality" does not mean holding on to this current body we inhabit. This is a mistaken notion. It means having a continuity of conscious awareness of our eternal nature whether we're in the process of dying, living, or being born.

This is the new revelation! *O Death where is thy sting? O grave, where is thy victory?* Therefore, our time of transformation is at hand. And we need to prepare for the world that is to come by being willing to move into the Great Unknown.

We understand now that the chasm, the void, or the Great Unknown is the giant collective Unconscious Mind, the uncreated side of all creation. It is also Jung's *pleroma* and the physicists' *unified field,* where spirit and matter, waves and particles, coexist in their contradictory natures. We'll be required to move forward consciously now, into this new way of being. But it's really not a new way at all; making it conscious is, and we will accomplish the current task by "being" it.

The sacralizing of this Planet Earth and humanity is a *real event in concrete reality*. We are all about to remember that we are immortal Sons and Daughters of God.

Immortality is recalled through soul-memory and the quality of expectation, literally a "re-called" future. This is an inner awakening, one that shifts and broadens our perspective, like putting on new glasses and seeing all of creation and ourselves through a wider, clearer lens.

Our species is reaching its fruition now; we are becoming the fully blossomed Human Being. This is an evolutionary fact. In our work at Eupsychia, we call this "arting ourselves." We are being newly formulated through a "simulation process"—consciously cooperating in our own evolution—becoming likened unto the image of a higher Self, our own Ideal. The archetypal realm and the human realm are merging to bring us this higher awareness of Humanity-as-One-Soul. Isn't this a thrilling prospect? Our task now is to heal ourselves and help usher in the means for the new kind of life awaiting us. There is no way to guarantee our success except through one method: We must *become* this new way ourselves. We must think anew, feel anew, and be as close to our Ideal as we can imagine. We collectively turn away from our past and narcissistic preoccupations. We do an "about-face" and together co-create the Future with focused intention.

The call has gone out, and the response has been heard. And because of this, we are standing on the brink of this whole new way of being, "hanging in the dangle" between two worlds, one that is dying and one that is being born—praying we'll all make it through. We are currently passing through a cycle of evolution that is taking our breath away. New energies of love for humanity can spin human nature through the most amazing shift in consciousness this planet has ever known. Something spiritual is happening right here on the time-line of our ordinary everyday reality. And we are all participating in this "high story," conscious of it or not. But it's more fun to do it consciously.

The needed reversal in our focus, from the outer world of appearances to the inner ways of spirit, began happening while we were otherwise preoccupied—for that's the nature of consciousness shifts. My physicist friend, Fred Alan Wolf, says that a paradigm shift is a quantum leap that happens the way a cloud reshapes into another cloud. You look away from the sky for a moment, and when you look back, though no time seemed to pass, *everything's different.*

So here we stand in the 1990s, vulnerable, curious, and fearful, for we no longer feel assured. We're being asked to do what human nature fears the most: to live in the midst of the unknown. Yet there's a sense of exhilaration and familiarity that makes this a time of enchantment and high spirits. As the intensity builds, we know we're on the brink of something vastly important. It's a leap from what has been to what could be. We're about to witness the shape-shifting of our world. As Christian mystic Tielhard de Chardin says:

> *Today, something is happening to the whole structure of human consciousness; a new kind of life is starting.*

When we come to the end of an age, larger patterns are activated within the psyche of humanity. The wheel of Life spins us through "a threshold time," an overlap between two worlds that are going in opposite directions. There are parallel universes, says Dr. Wolf, depending on what we recognize as real possibility. *Recognition* is the mental process that merges parallel universes.

A paradigm shift changes our entire worldview; it affects every aspect of our lives. We are placed on a brand new foundation, so we start all over with a higher consciousness. The shift in our world is not occurring outside of us; it is happening from within. As J. Krishnamurti recognized: "Our problems are in our consciousness, and not in the world." Our shift is one of *perspective*. And a transformation of the mind can happen instantly. We need to be open and willing to broaden our view, trusting and remembering what we already know deep within our hearts.

—

"THE EVOLUTIONARY MYSTIC":
THE BLEND OF SCIENCE AND SPIRITUALITY

This new consciousness is the shift to the inner life that mystics and spiritual paths have always proclaimed as the only way to reach God. And even more exciting, it moves us away from the "idol worship" of the purely objective sciences that invalidate the intuition and call our subjective life "unreal." For myself, I've recognized this change as my soul calling me home after some kind of grueling battle. I've often told my students that our bodies know truth and so do our souls; it's only our intellects that can lie. In the words of physicist John Hitchcock:

> *The intellect can bypass wisdom and consciousness like a motorcycle can a walker; it does so daily in every university. (1991: 251)*

Objective science and the rational intellect are excellent tools with know-how for constructing the scaffolds and designs that most efficiently contain and implement the ways of Spirit. But these outer formulations should come after intuitive experiences and emotional release have taken us to our true reality. Intellects are limited to data gathered from the past, and therefore they are incapable of being "wise" or "creative." These qualities can only come from the subjective life of the one who experiences it. No "outside

29

authority" can ever truly know us. And this is simply a fact, both physically and psychically.

The main difference between the dying and emerging worldview is this: In the old way, we thought we were standing apart from the evolutionary process, irrelevant objects in a mechanistic universe, acted upon by a greater force. Today, however, in studying the basis of human life, the field of subatomic physics has nixed this misconception. This exacting science has determined that

in observing a piece of data, the very act of observation *changes* it.

Our capacity to observe, it appears, is co-creating our personal reality at each moment in time. What we select to notice and believe from the pool of all possibilities is what we *will* see and give meaning as "real." "When you believe it, you'll see it." From our insights on this theory, we can now surmise that the observer indeed disturbs. Our consciousness itself, then, is creative, and we are responsible for what we create. Therefore, when many of us together believe in a similar worldview, a consensual reality is manifested.

Consciousness creates Reality, and we are all together this consciousness! We must now take full responsibility for the fact that *our thoughts are creative. We are the meaning-makers of our lives.*

The implications of this finding are profound concerning the nature of reality and the nature of human beings. You may want to stop and reflect for a moment on what this means. It implies we have a powerful role in our own evolution. We've been living in the middle of our own picture, unaware of the part we play in creation.

The contents of the collective unconscious mind are neutral until we assign them value through confrontation with our conscious mind. Consequently, we are the Reality-makers. The mind makes the leap. And a number of minds can change consensual reality. When there is a difference in our minds, the world is split up. When a merger occurs, simultaneous realities come to us—worlds come together— a reverberation.

Later, we'll see that what modern physics calls matter in the subatomic realm is what Carl Jung called the *pleroma* where all the archetypes, blueprints for all possible created things, reside. Looking "objectively" through the lens of science, it is the world of matter. Inside us at the deepest level, it may literally be our Creator's mind.

We are all the architects of the future.
When you have an inspiration, take note.
It may only come through once.

THE SYMBOLIC LEVEL OF REALITY:
COMING ALIVE WITH MEANING AND PURPOSE!

*And Jesus said to Nicodemus: Do not think carnally, or
you will be flesh, but think symbolically, and then you
will be spirit.*

—Jung's translation of John 3:3-7

Symbols are carriers of meaning and energy. They are
messengers between dimensions, bringing the language of a
higher order into the world just beneath it. They are the link
between two worlds that are interfacing.

To enter the symbolic life is to live in a higher reality. If
we view all our apparently unrelated outer conditions
through their symbolic meaning, grouping them into "meaningful clusters," we are making their sacred purpose visible.
In this fashion we spiritualize the material world. Rising
above our conditions like this is movement back to our
Source, where all patterns of wholeness, including that of
our own true Self, stand revealed. From this inner world of
meaning, we gain a bird's-eye view, rather than the myopic
view we have when living in the midst of it all.

The light of the intuition ignites when we make the commitment to live symbolically. We learn to read the keys from
symbolism and mythology. Then, we can apply these as
metaphors for our own personal lives and spiritual growth.
When I can see my Bigger Story that unfolds symbolically, I
feel immersed within the whole, which gratifies my need to
belong and is very fulfilling. Symbolic dreams and visions
begin to happen when we say, "Let there be light," and mean
it! From this higher vista, everything in life takes on an

archetypal quality. Things become "archetypal" when they reach the peak of their universal and perfect "type."

Archetypes are the time-honored divine blueprints of all things possible to create. They seek expression in modern-day garb through us in the concrete world. You can tell when something has taken on an archetypal significance by its intense transformative quality. It always feels "larger than life." Some of these Patterns enhance our lives, while others bring us great ordeals, illness, obstacles, or restrictions we must overcome. And all of this type of inner work is being used for the good of the whole as we move along toward learning to embody Spirit, or the Ideal, in human form.

Anytime we start on something new, we invoke the archetype of what we want to create. Most often, we do this unconsciously. But in this book, we'll be learning how to work consciously with the archetypal/creative dimension of our consciousness. It's one of our keynotes, in fact, because the doorway between our current world and this higher one is standing wide open, and it's up to us what we will create next. So learning of this matrix mind that resides in the human collective unconscious mind is perhaps the biggest key to our evolution.

Without a sense of meaning, material reality unfolds as if by a crooked, unpredictable line of chance events. The world of meaning is a better place to live than the world of seemingly random appearances. The illusions, glamour, and *maya* (appearances that look real but are only mirages) of the material life are not gratifying to the soul, unless they take on a higher meaning.

The Soul emanates from the formless world of the

Absolute. For it to enter into existence and be expressive, it must take form in the concrete life that we call ordinary reality. To achieve this aim, our Soul created a psyche as its double, or mirrored image, so it could see and feel itself as human. In so doing, an apparent dualism was born, the duality of spirit/matter. The psyche's "body" contains the entirety of both the conscious and unconscious mind, a storehouse for the "blueprints," or organizing Principles, around which we build all potential human qualities and experiences. Our psyche's "body" is made up of archetypal matrices, which activate and influence us from the collective unconscious mind anytime we focus on any one of the archetypes.

Whatever you are trying to work out in your life, there is always a symbolic/archetypal level of reality that matches it, containing the blueprint and the high story needed to carry out the creation. This is how the symbolic (or archetypal) level and the concrete level of reality interact for the sake of evolution. Every possible blueprint and script has a divine intent. And together, they all make up the essence of our God-nature, our whole and Absolute Identity.

These archetypal patterns manifest as either personages, qualities, or processes. To activate an archetypal pattern, we humans invoke it. This means we become fascinated by the attributes of a particular image, literally drawn into its "gravitational pull," and we thereby call it down as we rise up to resonate with its qualities. Something in us is matching (or hungering for) that "something" in the archetype, something we are longing for that will give meaning to our lives. Whenever we create a mental image of any of this primordial content, it becomes an ideal.

As you reflect upon a divine image or symbol of an ideal,

you will start to mold and be molded by its Pattern. Before you know it, you are experiencing signs of it manifesting in your life. And if you're not careful, you may go completely unconscious as these potent and numinous archetypal energies pour in. You can become obsessed with these high stories, or any one of the Images therein, and can fall into the very same "agony/ecstasy" duality these divine love affairs symbolize. The human psyche's Patterns are the "physical scaffolding" upon which the soul, our divine Self, comes into incarnation. Through this process, the ideal of anything can be realized in the ordinary world. We do not become the archetype, but we can become its representative here in this ordinary world.

When *all* of these preexistent psychic patterns are actualized, our psyche will manifest as the completed Self, or perfected Human Design. But remember, *perfected* means "completed."

COMPLEXES ARE SYMBOLIC/ARCHETYPAL, TOO

As you may already know from your experience, an archetypal pattern can get ahold of us, becoming a troublesome *complex*, in Freudian or Jungian terms, that overruns our ego's control and causes us to act out neurotically. Perhaps something is being exaggerated so we can "see" it more plainly. This is the function of archetypes: They force us to grow! At any rate, you know some lesson is in store when you sense you're being driven by a complex. Sometimes our Shadow, for instance, does something we don't even approve of and humiliates us in some grim fashion. Archetypes can play havoc with our lives if we go about this business of evolution unconsciously and ill-prepared. We all know what it feels like to become overly reactive for no apparent reason and act out automatically as though we have no conscious control over our behavior. We'll say, "Something just came over me." And this is true: We became overidentified with a Pattern of Wholeness—we tried to take on the whole thing.

Our task, then, and it can truly be intriguing, is to discover the empowering images beneath those intense feelings and emotions we have. And then we can access the particular archetype or aspect of divinity that is trying to express through us, capturing the larger meaning. If we accept this greater life as real, and choose to participate consciously in its creation, we are aiding in a Great Work: Two dimensions of consciousness are merging and progressing toward a whole new state of being, one never before realized. If we believe in evolution, we might even suspect that the archetypes are gridlocked in outworn patterns, too. They need us as we need them if we are to advance now. In the evolutionary process, this is the purpose of an "overlap" between two dimensions.

You can begin to follow these new, more silent and self-empowering principles that are showing up at both ends of the continuum of our human functioning—the basis of matter and the breadth of psyche. Self-knowledge is empowering, and it becomes wisdom if we actually practice what we learn. This book will help you recognize what is going on in the consciousness of all human beings at this critical time in the history of our personal and planetary evolution. It will give you a sense of playing a part in this great Cosmic Event. Rudolph Steiner, the esoteric Christian philosopher and founder of the philosophical school of anthroposophy, said that people who incarnate during the final twenty-five years of a major cycle are "a special breed" with a particular planetary mission to perform as bridge-builders into the New World. Somewhere within their experience, they are born already prepared for this task; they only need to awaken and take hold of the helm when they hear the inner call. For the soul truly never forgets its original intention and sacred purpose, even though our egos can certainly sleep through attempts to wake us.

Even though you may not quite remember who you truly are yet, you are being greatly affected by this "about face" in human consciousness. As we approach the millennium we are *all* filled with sacred hunger as we begin to spiral on and upward. Our appetites are getting voracious as we begin to sense our next step. Our new story is coming from the symbolic subjective realities. And we're all participating in its co-creation; each of us has a "sacred part" to fulfill.

Some of us are ready, even impatient, for the changes in store. Others, however, are rigidly holding on to the past, afraid for their very lives. And rightly so! For the old world is rapidly shape-shifting, and within this decade, it will gradually fade away. For those who continue to hold on so tightly, their transformation will be a bumpy ride. For those who are willing to "let go and let God," it will be a fabulous and heartfelt adventure! It's all up to you, and me, how we choose to do it. But let me tell you for certain: Given the state of our current evolutionary task at the closing of an age, no one will remain unchanged.

Chapter Three

DUALISM: OUR "HOLY GRIT"

All natures are good, yet just not good enough to prevent their badness from being equally obvious.
—*Carl Jung,* Aion

Humanity has always had to deal with conflicting pairs of opposites, maneuvering between shadow and light. As creatures of the Earth, it takes male and female aspects to conceive a child; religions teach us about good and evil. There is the ongoing battle between right and wrong, good and bad, winning or losing, I should/I shouldn't—either/or conflicts consume much of our emotional life. We've even been created under the influence of a double-helix DNA, the biophysical pattern for duality.

Our tendency is to get lost on one side of the polarity and remain resistant to the opposite side, leaving us in a state of "innocent" (unconscious) denial. But both sides of a polarity are real! When we repress the denied side of us into our unconscious, we tend to project our unwanted feelings, ideas, and behaviors onto those others we perceive as "the enemy" or "our problem." And obviously, as long we maintain unconsciousness of our dark side, we will be at war within, stuck in our process of becoming whole.

Dualism, then, is a *fact* built into our basic nature. And these opposites within are the "sparring partners," as Jung put it, that represent in some way every possible human dilemma. The battles between the dark and light within us become the issues that often shake us to our core, nearly wiping us out. They actually force us to seek a higher way. This friction between opposites is the creative force of nature, and therefore, of *our* nature as well. We realize these "warring opposites" must be part of God's plan for all of creation, including us. These complementary inner opposites are really "divine lovers" seeking always to unite in mutual respect and harmony.

So here we are, with this dark (and hidden, we hope) shadow side we deplore and refuse to own, and the ideal self-image we don for all to see. We tend to approve of ourselves when we've been "good" and feel disgust when we're "bad." And until we recognize that those two characters inhabiting this one body are one and the same creature, we're in trouble.

We think of this pull between the dark and the light side of us as something wrong—something we need to overcome. We try with all our might to be *only positive*. This seems like a good idea, but unfortunately, it doesn't work. Here are some of the dualities we must understand about ourselves, and integrate:

Soul - Human
Masculine - Feminine
Good - Evil
Spirit - Matter
Heavenly - Earthly

Religion - Psychology
Animal - Human
Positive - Negative
Discarnate - Incarnate
Uncreated - Created
Evolution - Involution
Human - Superhuman
Archetypal - Instinctual
Wisdom - Knowledge
Right - Wrong
Wholeness - Fragments
Future - Past
Wave - Particle

Take some time now to look over this list, and reflect on where you stand on each issue they represent in your life. Are you comfortable and accepting of these "splits," or is your psyche still dealing with them as active, warring oppositions?

THE OPPOSITES WITHIN ARE LOVERS

Our complementary opposites play an important role in our journey of Becoming. They are all part of us and we are a product of them, both sides. Like two sides of one coin, each polarity has its unique and contrary nature. Together they make a whole. These inner pairs of opposites all function as "lovers" seeking to unite. The attraction of the opposites for one another is great, and the tension between them, while they are held apart, is enormous. When we integrate these opposites, the tension dissolves and we move into a new consciousness beyond our dualistic state. This law of

41

complementarity runs throughout all the created universe.

We'll learn more about the human shadow and the nature of addiction later, for it is all connected to the duality with which we live—loving some parts of ourselves while hating others. Further along, we'll explore how our shadow developed in our early years and the pathway we can follow to reclaim our whole nature, both the dark side and the light, so we can live a more fulfilled life with less inner conflict.

AN EVER-EXPANDING VIEW OF GOD

This core duality is God-given, residing not only in human nature, but in the divine, our Creator-God. A quick glance at the Bible will cause a reader to conclude that God is not only a loving Father, His wrathful side brought many of our ancestors to their knees.

In the Old Testament, for instance, God was the Almighty Powerful, said to punish us when we were "bad." Humans bowed in fear of this God. In the New Testament, God became His Son, The Christ, a loving God-in-Human-form who we could access as more like ourselves. Today, we are aware of the God-within, the Immanent God of theology, unfolding a new understanding of divinity for us to experience and love. Carl Jung's view of God might be extremely helpful for us now, as it seems to fit perfectly with what we know of our own nature.

When we search for the God-within, we must deal with the laws of the psyche, for, as the mind who perceives and images (imagines) the world, the psyche is the mediator between spirit and matter. Human history is replete with the horrors that an unhealthy, unconscious psyche creates in the name of God—indeed, a bogus spirituality.

Jung's concept of the God-Image is the Self we find within our own psyche. Many of us perceive Christ as the archetypal Self in dreams and times of meditation and introspection. In one sense, The Christ is an *icon*, representing God the Father on Earth. From our vantage point now, The Christ also becomes the archetype for the fully blossomed Human, the Son of Man, as He always called Himself. He made a journey of ascension in the body—making this possibility real for humanity—the purpose of an archetype.

This phenomenon is backed by science in Rupert Sheldrake's discovery:

> *Once a single member of a species accomplishes something for the first time, a place in the collective consciousness is made for all others to follow; a new possibility has been established that we can image as fact. You may have heard this concept expressed as "the hundredth monkey syndrome." (1981)*

The maxim "As above, so below" is the universal Law of Correspondence. It states that if we can know something of the nature of a molecule, we can know something of the nature of God. Truth, on any level of consciousness, is consistent. Jung's perception of God came from his study of the biblical figure, Job, The story of Job caused Jung to conclude that God's "light of love glows with a fierce dark heart.... He is a complex of coincidental opposites" (1973: para. 664). "God is not only to be loved, but also to be feared" (para. 747). "It is quite right, therefore, that fear of God should be considered the beginning of all wisdom" (para. 664).

So you see, when we begin tracing "the warring opposites" back through the history of our species, we discover a dualism running throughout our nature, all the way to the heights of a fearsome and loving God.

Jung's deep quest concerning the nature of God brought us an understanding of a psychic law that will govern the coming times concerning our relationship to our Maker and to our own co-creative nature: the Law of Antinomy. This will enable us, for the first time, to dissolve our dualism. As Jung points out:

> *Yahweh is not split but is an antinomy—a totality of inner opposites—and this is the indispensable condition for his tremendous dynamism, his omniscience and omnipotence.* (Answer to Job, para. 567)

The contradictory nature of our lives reflects the nature of reality. Jung's point of view, "All opposites are of God," is validated in physics by the law of complementarity. When an entity behaves as both *form* and *wave function* (creature and God force), the entity or whole contains both within its nature. This is duality within unity, or *the opposites contained within the One* (Hitchcock 1991).

So how do we relate to our opposing forces—our contradictory nature? At the archetypal level, our human psyche, made in God's image, encompasses these contradictory characteristics without problem. Integrated opposites are part of our wholeness pattern at the psyche's level of reality. There, opposites are building blocks to our nature, not obstacles at all in their unmanifest state. But when existing in our ordinary human reality, they become our "afflictions of soul." To make complementary what was, while unconscious, conflictual, is a shift that automatically creates transcendence of a troublesome pattern. Once this process is thoroughly understood, we can learn to make this shift at will. You may want to ponder this for a while. There is a great secret here.

All our essential steps in the awakening of our consciousness stem from this searing battle of opposites. Obstacles are in our way of being in the divine flow. Yet these obstacles are what force us to make the conflicts conscious. Light cannot be seen until it strikes an object! For humans, becoming conscious *is* suffering. *But suffering is not the goal; deepening into Life is.* As Joseph Campbell once said, it's not so much the meaning of life that we seek intellectually, but more "the rapture of being alive."

Therefore, the sacred purpose of the shadow is plain. The shadow in us will keep us aware of the unredeemed parts of ourselves, those parts we're in denial of that hold our passions and dynamism. For our wholeness, *all* our unconscious elements must be made conscious. And becoming fully conscious and living enraptured is our true purpose in this divine human experiment.

Psyche, our human soul, manifested herself on the mental plane upon the ladder of evolution to perform this function. She is a scaffold upon which spiritual force is molded into form. She brings to us, either through "symptom" or "symbol," as much Reality as we can handle at any one time. Our egos either surrender to this high and holy work, or they resist and cause us great strain. *All human suffering is an inability for the soul to express its true nature, which is service, in this world.*

—

THE PARADIGM SHIFT IN A NUTSHELL

As you go forward now in the study of what's to come, you can synthesize the paradigm shift into two major transformative events we're now required to undergo. These are our current evolutionary tasks:

- Making a shift from hating one side of ourselves while loving the other, to accepting our nature of opposites; learning to work with the dynamism of the opposites to *activate and fuel creativity*. This will dissolve our dualism.

- Making a shift from a disease-based psychology to viewing our symptoms as birthing a new consciousness. This will end our low self-esteem, returning to us our soul powers and our spiritual purpose. This *releases our creative expression*.

Now we are rethinking our basic understanding of who we are and how we heal and grow. We must learn to stand within the tension of the opposites, no matter how much we feel pulled this way or that. Our philosophy must change from *either/or* to *both/and*. To do this, we must sacrifice our attachment to judge, compete, and divide ourselves into "I'm right and you are wrong," "This part of me is 'good,' this part 'bad.'" From now on, we must always remember that we are both matter and spirit, both ego and soul. And each aspect of our nature is divine. We are a hybrid species—part of God's divine plan for evolution. And all our activities are sacred works, designed for the good of the whole. But we need to know who we are healing before we can help the Self evolve. If our psychotherapies and treatment programs are based on the assumption that we are only egos, we can never truly heal. The great Indian sage, Sri Aurobindo, offered us the key when he cautioned us that

> *the significance of the lotus is not to be found by analyzing the secrets of the mud from which it grows; its secret is to be found in the heavenly archetype of the lotus that blooms forever in the Light above. (qtd. in Satprem 1968)*

We are not in need of "fixing," not sick or inferior, but undergoing the crisis of a natural birth. Birthing a new consciousness will require a complete ego death to the old ways that have always held our identities together. We've labeled ourselves in ways that make us feel bad, wrong, damaged, sick, or insane. And this has kept us stuck in shame, low self-esteem, and blame. It has kept us from taking responsibility for ourselves and our lives. Now it's time to look in a new direction, and learn about our transformation.

Our evolutionary tasks will become quite clear when we make the ultimate identity shift that will change us forever—the ultimate Self-remembrance:

We are not human beings learning to be spiritual; we are spiritual beings learning to be human.

THE PURPOSE OF THE OPEN HEART

To behold with the eyes of the Heart; to listen with the ears of the Heart to the roar of the world; to remember the culmination of the past through the Heart, thus must one impetuously advance upon the path of ascent.

—Agni Yoga Teachings, Heart

The open heart holds the key to our current transformation. It is where the ego and the soul meet for their divine union. This open heart is the gateway between dualism and the unity of our nature.

The transpersonal/personal Heart is the archetype that functions as the Divine "alchemist" of the human organism. This is the meeting place of the lower and higher emotions. For example, we would feel devastated at the death of a loved one, but at the same time we might feel radiating joy for this person's release and the special significance this one life had in the world. Both personal and transpersonal feelings unite during times of extreme heartbreak—passion and compassion unite.

In my own life, I was once suffering greatly during a therapy session about the plight of my first-born, diabetic son, who has had a trying physical life. I was deeply into the personal aspect: Why him, why me? And I was gripping my stomach as I wailed out my grief. Suddenly, within my consciousness I was aware that I was soaring over Planet Earth and seeing all the mothers at once who had sick children or who had lost a child. I felt united with all mothers of the world. It was a blessed moment of intense relief. I am not being singled out! This, too, is just another human experience, affecting all of us at some time or another. The personal and symbolic/archetypal had come together so I could transcend. I had experienced the bigger meaning, the spiritual significance of our plight.

Pleasure and pain are one in bliss. Denying neither one or the other—*this* is the activity of the Heart. This "divine tension" of the Heart keeps us in touch with our whole nature, our joys and our sorrows together; and the two become a third and higher entity. Neither seeking one nor wallowing in the other—this is the emotional freedom of bliss!

No matter how our lives are divided into good and evil, pleasure or pain, it is all part of the Divine Plan for us to become aware that we are inherently divine. If you'll reflect on this for a minute, it will become clear. Humanity has to "fall" in order to "rise." We have to leave the nest, acting out our creation story again and again, both separately as individual egos and collectively as one Soul, until we are conscious of our true nature.

Chapter Four

PSYCHOSPIRITUAL INTEGRATION

As the twentieth century comes to a close, we human beings find ourselves moving through a significant time of transition. The call grows stronger every day to let go of our old, limited patterns of thinking and behaving so that we can embrace the new, more harmonious ways of living in the world. We are being urged from within to die to the past and be resurrected.

—*Yogi Amrit Desai*

THE BLENDING OF OUR HUMAN/SPIRITUAL NATURES:
HUMANITY'S EVOLUTIONARY TASK AT THE CLOSING OF AN AGE

You are being called now to come into your highest expression—to rise fully into "the light of your own soul" and to stand for what you know as Truth. Your time of completion is here! If this is your truth, you will resonate with this message. If not, then that's okay, too. You will, however, hear others in your life speaking of this "call." Perhaps this book will help you relate to them. Now, if this is your truth, the knowledge you require is going to come quite rapidly as you learn to look within: One small moment of accessing this numinous inner wholeness brings you back in touch with your soul's original purpose for incarnation, reminding you once more of your true life's work and spiritual significance.

Your spiritual nature is a psychological fact. It is the real and transformative force that empowers your life. To deny this core nature of yours is to deny your very Self.

A process of "psychospiritual integration" begins to occur naturally when the ego and soul turn to focus upon one another. When this happens, we've landed at the gateway of the heart. A cry goes out from the hungry and fretful ego, having gone to the edge of its own power. It reaches up toward spirit, and a response is heard from the soul, from the subjective world of the vast collective unconsciousness, in touch with the Greater Story. The soul descends to meet its concretized counterpart with a feeling of compassion and love. As we open our hearts in a willing and accepting attitude, our process of purification begins.

So at first, all hell breaks loose! For as we've already seen through our bare beginnings here, the two aspects of our nature are opposite from one another and complement each other: feminine/masculine, earthy/airy, dark/light, personal/transpersonal, dense/transparent, intense/light-hearted—in form as in spirit. Obviously, there would be great upheaval at first, as the two consciously enter one body. Many people, in fact, never even make it to this point of their process of individuation, that of becoming an effective psychospiritual human in the world, an undivided "in-dividual."

When you first invoke a spiritual quality, you can learn to be specific concerning the particular "brand" that will best balance your personality. Then, I must warn you: You'll attract to yourself the tests that will best train you for this new skill! Your body/ego will undergo whatever purification it must to become similar to the ideal you've demanded. You'll probably be put through an ordeal of experiencing its opposite at first. Therefore, it can feel worse instead of better at the start. For example, if "patience" is what you name as balancing an overly active impetuous nature, you'll be showered with opportunities that try your patience to the hilt while your impetuousness is refined.

The soul's main task is to aid humanity in dissolving dualism, helping it learn to live within the tension of the complementary opposites within its own nature.

The task of psychospiritual integration, then, is to honor the dual aspects of our nature, the ego and the soul, the past and the future life, and to see that all are sacred and arise from out of the same life stream, the whole. In this type of personal work, we are adopting Tielhard de Chardin's definition of us as "spirit-matter" who can never be split into an "either/or." To deny our human feelings or our divine heritage—either one—will lead us into a cul-de-sac of nongrowth and, quite possibly, the repetition of some old painful lesson in living. Both aspects are necessary for the "wholing" of the psychospiritual Self.

To awaken means to become fully responsible and consciously participate in our own personal and collective unfoldment. This natural evolutionary process happens all by itself; we simply learn to get out of its way and cooperate with the larger patterns that are influencing us from within. To assume responsibility for "our part" of this co-creative process, we have to turn inward and seek our truth from within our own nature. Otherwise, we're just doing the same old inauthentic thing: living our lives by the borrowed truths of others' ideas and beliefs about how everything "ought to be," and depending on their bias on how we "ought to heal."

Sometimes, of course, others can be our guides; for their way of viewing things tracks with our direct experience and validates what we are getting for ourselves. Yet, as we know only so well, many of these external theories are just "talk," and only match someone else's intellectual constructs that may appear logical, and worked for *them*, but do not necessarily speak to us or move us into new ways of being.

Accessing higher potentials within ourselves begins by asking. We start by recognizing these higher dimensions of human consciousness as *real*, thereby giving them meaning. Anything we make real in such a way then has permission to move in and impact our psyches, but not otherwise! On this planet, we have free will, so anything coming from a higher Source must have our permission to interfere with our lives. This answers that age-old question concerning prayer: "Well, if God already knows everything, then He knows what we need. So why do we need to pray?" Our asking is the key! This is how co-creation works. We do it through a process called "invocation," which is how conscious co-creators pray.

THE POWER OF INVOCATION:
THE CALL GOES OUT; THE RESPONSE IS HEARD

The words *invocation* and *evocation* describe a mysterious emanation, a voiceless appeal representing an inherent urge toward freedom. This yearning to transcend a condition is innate in every species. It concerns interplay and relationship with two dimensions of consciousness when a shift is needed toward a higher way. As a plant pushes toward the sun, and a child extricates itself from parental influence, we, as a species, push toward the transcendence of our nature into that of the divine Life. Ultimately, this "sacred hunger" causes us to unite with our highest blueprint, bringing our completion.

Invocation is how we access a higher order when we choose to participate consciously in our own evolution. When we choose to invoke our Higher Power, we are taking a stand as co-creators in the Divine Plan. We can either do this consciously now and awaken, or unconsciously, as we've done in the past. But participate, we do! So we may as well take responsibility for our part and not simply toss ourselves chaotically into the rapidly spinning spirals of fate.

INVOCATION IS CO-CREATIVE PRAYER

Invoking is *active* prayer, a self-assertive way to pray that lacks the passive religious connotations. In the past, prayer was our approach, but this was an emotional appeal, more of a plea of helplessness, asking that God come into our lives and help us. Common prayer often is predicated on the notion that we are weak and ineffectual creatures at the mercy of an external god not related to us at all. Invocation is prayer for the Aquarian Age, where Self-empowerment is our keynote; it is a co-creative appeal to a Higher Power, indicating we're ready and eager to do our part, as Spirit's hands and feet. The power of invocation gives us a position of strength, yet we know that we don't have the power to create high qualities apart from our God-nature. We invoke them and make a commitment to enact these divine powers through our body/ego as they surface within us from our Source. This is what the co-creation truly means. It is a demand: "Send me my instructions! I am willing to take the ball and run."

POINTS OF ATTAINMENT ALONG THE ROAD

These points of attainment along our road gradually merge our inner aspirations and our outer expression into one life, the building blocks of embodying spirit. These psychospiritual tasks are initiatory in quality, for they each bring us into a new part of ourselves. They each contain a lesson in the balancing of the opposites. They are "trials by fire" that when mastered become great powers we can wield, in love and truth. Though somewhat ordered and hierarchical, these psychospiritual goals do not necessarily come in a linear way. There are fourteen "tasks" or "intentions" briefly described in what follows. In studying these, you may discover more on your own.

1. We enter onto the Path. Through pain and suffering, or some sort of bottoming out, we begin to release our preoccupation with the outer world of appearances and turn inward to a way that is more fitting for our nature.

Unfortunately, most of us take this step only after extreme devastation. But it doesn't have to be this way: We can learn from our observation of life and the trials we've already overcome, to consciously choose this less traveled inner way.

At this first stage of our journey as conscious co-creators, we sacrifice our attachment to the illusions we've held within the world of appearances. We stop old dysfunctional behaviors and watch ourselves instead of acting out. Keeping a journal of our desires and insights, using a friend or group for support, or going into therapy, are very helpful at this critical stage of our awakening. We have the courage now to say to our inner God:

Let Reality govern my every thought and Truth be the master of my life!

And it does require courage to state this affirmation: It will bring down any illusory aspect of your life, sometimes in one fell swoop! We are tempted no longer by superficial distractions. They bore us. We learn to separate the wheat from the chaff and turn away from things that have no ultimate meaning for us. This is a test of faith.

2. We recognize our true nature. As we begin to trust this inner way, through our own experience of it (for there is no other way to know this path), we begin to realize that we've always known the truth, that we are made in the image of our Creator-God, that we are more than what we appear to be. We see that we don't have to learn a lot of new things; we only need to remember ourselves and why we are here.

As inner miracles unfold, and we begin to meet others of like intention, we feel heartened, and we become more certain that our nature is both human and divine.

3. We face and embrace our shadow self. The shadow is the easiest of the archetypes to access. It won't leave us alone until we face it! Therefore, we must "enter into that narrow door" and turn ourselves over to the process of accepting our dark and unloved side. This does require inner work, and usually even some humiliation. But in the midst of loving company of others like ourselves, who are also doing inner work, we can come out of denial about our undeveloped and unconscious side.

4. We reenter our past and release its hold on us. Anyone who inhabits a body has unfinished business from the past. When we enter the path, it's as though a wise intelligence shines a light into the dark closets of our subconscious minds. We are commanded to reenter these old storage bins and dredge up any unresolved emotions or situations that still need to be forgiven. Forgiving is divine forgetting, and for this activity, there is no quick fix available; it is a process.

Forgiveness means to reenact the original "insults," with the objectivity now of the observer self. As we shine the light back into our past, we see not only our helplessness and innocence, but also the ignorance and causes in the lives of those who harmed us. And from our more lofty view, we can see how it all made sense, having come from painful and constrictive fear, the wrong side of love. We begin to see the Bigger Picture. Forgiving ourselves and others for their mistakes and ignorance releases us. It's not about letting others off the hook; they still must face their own errors and harmful ways. Forgiveness is about setting ourselves free of the past.

5. *We refine our personalities.* As we start to forget our past, we have more free attention to place on the status of our unfolding Self. We begin to invoke qualities of that Ideal that lives in our heads and hearts, that one we are longing to be. And as it begins to show itself within our subjective life, we start to take this identity on. As we do, our old "parts" begin to dissolve, and we are changed. First we'll notice that the same old things no longer bother us. Next we'll begin to notice that our outward appearance changes. People who haven't seen us for a while will stop us with statements like, "What's happening to you? You look so different." Then, before we know it, we'll be acting and living more as the newer, more integrated Self.

Lessons will appear in life everywhere we need refining. As we undergo the lessons consciously, we'll learn for ourselves which parts we wish to hold on to and which parts we need to release. No one else can decide that for us.

Along with this refinement process, our life's purpose and true talents become visible. At first, we might not believe it. Could we really be so special that we might have a talent or two? Something worthwhile to offer back to the Life that gives us so much?

Yes. Yes. We start to evidence the aspects of our nature that fit with our life's mission and true purpose. Yet we see that much stuff is still in our way. So we follow ideas and practices, programs or therapies that are self-actualizing. We begin to take our own healing and inner work seriously.

And these opportunities will present themselves as if by magic, too. Our commitment and spiritual intention provide the key. Now, you may take this last sentence lightly, but let me say it again, so you will truly hear: Your spiritual intentionality will from this point forward be determining your life! And all your choices! Either consciously or unconsciously. This is the way of a spiritual aspirant and the nature of this path. Once the commitment is sound, there is no turning back: Your personality will be purified, and your life will be transformed.

6. We resolve the mystery of death/rebirth. As our inner work begins to unfold and we start to heal, we gain insights into how we actually grow and evolve. We see that when we are on a path of direct experience, we do not grow by becoming better every day; we grow through cycles of symbolic death/rebirth events in the subjective life. And we learn there are predictable stages to how we move through time and into higher dimensions. At times, we'll be preconscious, involved in a "participation mystique"—meaning we aren't even aware that we are transforming; we feel peaceful and all is well. Nothing needs to be questioned.

Then we enter a stage where we may feel depressed or stuck. And we'll feel hopeless, maybe even despairing, and our dream begins to die. We think at first that something is wrong with us, that we've perhaps done it all wrong. A process is urging us forward, but we've dug in our heels and won't budge; we don't trust it anymore. We may sleep a lot, or act out in ways to distract ourselves. But we still get nowhere; we go down instead of up. Others seem to be getting ahead of us, and we feel we are losing our life. How did this happen, we ask? Things had seemed to be going fine, when suddenly the picture changed. Not only do we feel we are dying inside, our outer life may become a mirrored reflection of death; we may begin to lose what we love the most—our friends, livelihood, possessions, even a sense of ourselves.

This is the stage of the birth process we all hate the most: metaphorically, it is when the mother's body has started labor, but the fetus doesn't feel prepared, and certainly doesn't know what to do about it. The actual process of "pushing through" is still premature. In this stage, we are building force for what is to come next, and it is indeed an uncomfortable stage in any transformation process.

Then, the pangs of birth get so strong we get angry! The process is relentless and our rage accelerates. This rage is the greatest gift! It is this impetus, in fact, that pushes us on through the metaphoric birth canal and unblocks us. The energy we have at this stage of our process is superhuman; we are capable of bursting through all types of resistance. We are coming through into a new dimension of consciousness, breaking out of our cocoon. This part of the process is charged with the energies of transformation, and is often chaotic. There is no other way to get born; we must surrender to the process.

7. We learn to live within the tension of the opposites. Now that we are becoming more familiar with the terrain of Self-knowledge and transformation, we see that our personality's desires and outer situations are always going to shift around, and much of it is truly beyond our control. We live in a world that is imbalanced. Instability rules us in every area of our lives, and as our moods go up and down, our minds are not always clear and decisive. We sometimes churn every which way in the watery world of feelings.

Instead of getting bent out of shape about this unpredictable state of affairs, giving ourselves self-talk of hopelessness and despair, we can begin watching ourselves more precisely. Our observer self comes to the foreground as a major player in our transformation. We realize that we do indeed live amid the tension of the warring opposites. They are all around us and within us as well. So how do we work with this? The mystery unfolds: We see that when we're too low, instead of waiting for the other shoe to drop, we can shift our focus to the positive side of the polarity and practice doing what will bring about our dream. Through disciplining our minds and focusing on projects that excite us, we don't give the negative side a chance to overwhelm us anymore.

When we feel too high or outrageously positive, we'll start to notice that we are falling into a state of inauthenticity. Our aggravations, doubts, and irritations are being repressed to the point that we can become depressed. Panic can even set in. So we let some of the negativity out in safe ways—perhaps even in private ways—that do no harm to another. We balance by taking a short inventory of what we feel and of what we may be denying. The key is to stay in the middle and hold the tension of both sides at once in balance!

We learn to sit in the middle of the seesaw, balancing out the extremes. From the center we can wield the power of the Self, who is above it all and doesn't need to fear for its life; the Self is eternal. Our task is to let the extremes come and go, while we refuse to buy into the forces of either side, never for a moment forgetting who we are.

8. We recognize our fellow travelers. Along this path of the heart we meet many soul brothers and sisters. There is an instant recognition when one comes along. Instead of isolating and protecting our egoistic stances (as we used to do), we begin to share our real feelings, discoveries, and new quest with others who are truly interested. We provide each other with context and validation for our new and expanding realties.

These new friends don't have to be with us geographically all the time; they are with us even when we are miles apart. These are true relatives; we are connected through the heart. Even though we may never all meet each other face to face, our work is cumulative. We may begin to network, team up on projects that excite us, love and support one another, and help uphold the fragile new worldview that is appearing on the horizon of our minds. We see that we are a group soul, with a higher purpose than our mere personal lives. As we expand, our world expands. The greatest blessing of all: Now we know for certain that we are never alone.

9. We awaken to our life's work and soul's expression. This happens spontaneously through opportunities that open to us. Joseph Campbell said he'd noticed that when people "follow their bliss," doors open. This is true! We never have to think too much about how we are going to serve in this world. It's as though the world comes to us and asks us to become involved through the specific avenues for which we're already cut out. We've been preparing all our lives for our life's mission; we've just not realized this. Your life's work will always be in the areas where you are comfortable, talented, fascinated, and feel the most at home.

If you are saying, *But I haven't found my way yet; my life's work is still unrevealed,* then be patient; have faith and perseverance. You are still in training in some ways you may not recognize. Eventually you will be led through that golden door to your long-awaited dream. Often your greatest advances happen when you least expect them, generated from events that had seemed just ordinary or insignificant at the time.

10. We learn to relax and be ourselves. Even when you feel you are tenuously "hanging in the dangle" between old ways that are dead and new ways that haven't quite arrived, you can practice being yourself. This will guarantee that you won't get off the mark again by accepting some job or recreation that isn't truly for you. Impatience is a hurdle we all have to overcome. Self-doubt and impetuous decisions are two of the enemies we must challenge and tame as we undergo this inward journey. We can practice their complementary qualities, which will, of course, balance them.

This will bring a state of bliss and relaxation. This is not a passive state, devoid of feeling. This is living within the intensity of the zero point between two potent forces, holding them at bay while we are both full and empty simultaneously. Fully relaxing is living from the heart. With nothing to hide, and nothing from which to run, we are authentic. There is no urgency to distract us.

11. We express our spiritual gifts and talents in the world of ordinary activities. Expression of our true life's work and sacred mission expresses our essence. Whatever forms this takes is perfectly okay with your Creator-God. Of this, I am quite certain.

Your life's work is simply that of "doing your Being"; it does not matter how or where.

12. We continually follow the mystery... We can never know where the Future will lead us. We only know we are willing, and we are not naive! We've seen how we sometimes have to die to entire ways of being, to our old identities. As we go along, we trust that this is God's creative expression. The beautiful thing about following a mystery is that you are always intrigued. Tell me, now, would you ever want it any other way? Not me!

If anyone tells you they know what exactly the future will bring, they are not telling you the truth. What we are about to experience has never been conceived by anyone on this planet. Nor anywhere else. Otherwise, the stories of all the religions of the world have been a lie, and I don't believe that for a minute! We must *be* what we want for the future. With faith, and patience, and a lot of perseverance we follow the mystery, until we reach Home. Then, we start out again.

13. ...until we develop continuity of consciousness. Continuity of consciousness is immortality's real name. We become conscious of our process, whether that is the process of birthing, living on a certain level of consciousness, or dying.

When I was twenty-nine years old, I was having a

miscarriage (my second in a row) and was hospitalized while hemorrhaging dangerously. At one point, in my hospital room, I was aware that I was on the ceiling looking down at my body on the bed. I had lost so much blood, my life was leaving. While on the ceiling, I realized my consciousness had expanded beyond the confines of that poor little weak body lying there on the bed. I had compassion for Jacquie Sue, but I was coolly deciding whether or not to reenter that body. As a "clinical near-deather," I do not *believe* in an afterlife; I *know* the first stages of the afterlife. Our consciousness we experience as "me" never leaves us, no matter what is going on.

When we become conscious of all levels at once, we know we are immortal. We know *experientially* that there is no beginning and no end. For according to *The Gospel of St. Thomas* from the Dead Sea Scrolls

> when we make the inner and the outer one, and the above as the below...then shall we enter the kingdom.

Now, tell me: Do you recall not ever being? Think about it. I bet you've always been. I have.

14. We take responsibility for being planetary citizens and leaders in our specific area of influence. We must pass the final threshold into our ultimate ordeal: that of overcoming all self-doubt. Self-doubt is the antithesis of remembering who we are. It remains with us, until it doesn't anymore. There is nothing we can do about it but recognize it when we have it. By remaining conscious of the fact that doubt is our greatest barrier to Self-realization, it gradually loses its hold on us.

When you find yourself with feelings of self-doubt or low self-esteem, *you can stop. Go within. Center. Turn your attention to the other side of the seesaw. And contemplate what Self-remembering is. Then you can begin to allow a picture to form in your mind's eye of your completed and Ideal Self. Then notice the feelings that come with being this Self. Gradually, now, notice your Self enter you from within and come fully through your personality.*

When you become your Self, your sacred hunger will abate. A higher, more integrated "I" now walks along "the middle way," going about its sacred business of balancing all extremes and spiritualizing the material world. We learn to live in moderation and nonattachment, the message both The Buddha and The Christ brought to the world, to "be in the world and not of it." A brand new archetype, the Self, will make itself present and visible on the Earth, through you and me.

HUMAN PSYCHOLOGY TAKES "THE LEAP"

The literal meaning of *psychology* is "the study of the soul." Therefore, it's logical now to include our deeper, more spiritual self as legitimate for study. During these nonordinary times in human history (I call them "destiny moves"), nonordinary approaches are necessary to get to the truth of the entirety of the human situation. We have to look wider to see the overview. The emerging schools of psychology are psychospiritual in nature. As we come through the final decade of this millennium, modern psychology is making a U-turn from involving to evolving, from outer to inner focus. In a nutshell, psychology is having to expand because human beings are!

Chapter Five

HARVESTING THE GOODS FROM OUR PAST

It's not revolution; it's evolution.
—Shawn Phillips

Before we go further into various aspects of our new understanding and new worldview, the evolution of the field of psychology can help us get a clearer perspective. Let's go back through our history for a while so we can recognize the new spiritual psychology and timely importance of our psychospiritual integration.

Our world is shape-shifting as rapidly as are our minds. We're moving up the evolutionary ladder toward more integrated and expansive definitions of the Self on its journey toward completion as One Humanity. It is beyond our scope here to provide a complete historical account of all the stages we've come through in the search for human understanding, but here is a mental springboard to view the emerging paradigm of human psychology more clearly, with a holistic perspective.

With humanity on the brink of a new way of being, our ways of viewing human nature and how we heal are changing. This is truly a major shift! An emerging psychology of wholeness is legitimatizing both the ego and beyond-ego levels of human functioning. These now are recognized not only by mystics of the world, but also by modern science and the developing field of transpersonal and spiritual psychology. The "beyond ego" levels of human functioning fall into the domain of the soul, or Higher Self—in Carl Jung's language, the Self.

Even the field of medicine, the most exacting of the sciences, is rapidly transforming, from behavioral medicine and its "mind/body" connection to complementary medicine, honoring both traditional and alternative healing. Medicine has expanded beyond recognizing only the "physical" as real, exploring the role of emotional, interpersonal, and spiritual components in healing life-threatening physical diseases.

We now know that guided imagery can change our conditions and our bodies' reactions to them. We are finding that "nonlocal prayer" can help heal us. Articles have been published in professional journals on a ground-breaking system of healing—transpersonal medicine. Physician and author Larry Dossey has developed a model, Era III Medicine, that moves consciousness and the ability to heal beyond the confines of the individual physical body and brain, asserting that the Mind cannot be completely localized. This approach validates intercessory prayer, long distance healing, noncontact diagnoses, and miracles as legitimate phenomena for analysis and research. It postulates that we humans are part of an interconnected whole, and that we have the ability to affect one another nonlocally. This is one more example of the expanding knowledge of the psyche. It goes beyond the past limitations we have attributed to it, tracking with the findings in the field of modern physics.

PSYCHOLOGY AND ITS EVER-EXPANDING VIEW OF THE SELF

To understand the emerging spiritual psychology, it's helpful to review the four distinct forces or major schools of human psychology that have come before. Each brought unique contributions to the new paradigm that carries us into the third millennium. Each school has offered great insights for our advancement, as well as pitfalls and limitations. And each has been a major force in influencing how we view human nature and how it heals.

Transpersonal psychology—the Fourth Force and cutting edge of human psychology—represents a refined synthesis of all that has come before, along with its own unique attributes. Many students of human psychology believe it is the bridge to an understanding of the Self. You might say now is our time to experience "a psychology of completion" as we pass through this final decade of the century. As we mature as a human species, our experience of who we are shifts into a greater and higher identity, until at some point we identify with the whole Self, our core nature. So now, for just a while, let's look back at how we got to this point.

FIRST FORCE PSYCHOLOGY: FREUDIAN PSYCHOANALYSIS

First Force psychology was founded by Sigmund Freud, whose name has become a household word. This great doctor's philosophies of the ego are still determining the parameters by which most people, consciously or unconsciously, judge whether someone is mentally healthy or not.

You often hear people humorously say, "I need to see a shrink," when they begin to feel the symptoms of mental or emotional strain.

Psychiatrists, who are medical doctors, are still, in many people's opinions, the only qualified experts in the area of our minds. Some people do not realize there are other helping professionals who are even better trained as psychotherapists: clinical social workers, addiction counselors, pastoral counselors, marriage and family therapists, and school counselors are often more effective in creating a therapeutic milieu and rapport with their clients.

But Dr. Freud brought humanity a great gift: He taught us to respect the power of the unconscious mind and to realize that most of our human strivings and behavior are unconsciously motivated. He taught that we needed to look deep within the psyche to discover the causative levels of our thoughts, feelings, impulses, and actions. His school of thought classified the ego, the superego, and the id as the three divisions of the human psyche that, when they are cooperating and when their workings are made conscious to their host, produce a normally functioning, well-balanced human being. The ego is viewed as the executor of our personality, and the ruler of our conscious life. In this book, we retain Freud's understanding of this function of the ego, as the gate-keeper between our conscious and unconscious minds.

Freud viewed our unconscious mind as a personal repository for all our forgotten and repressed contents, a gathering place within our psyche for all the emotional and psychic material that has cropped up in our lives—material too potent or threatening for us to handle. Therefore, when an unconscious process became activated by an outer stimulus that reminded our psyche of this old wound, an unconscious reaction beyond the control of our ego would pop out, acting out inappropriately in our lives, often causing us much difficulty.

For example, I may have been abused by a tall, red-haired uncle in my early childhood. Yet having no conscious memory of this fact, because I've repressed the entire subject, I overreact to every tall red-haired man I meet, even to a stranger matching this description. This might not present any problem unless this current red-haired man is my boss, or my husband's father, or someone with whom I need to have a significant relationship.

The medical model in our modern human sciences owes much of its genesis to Sigmund Freud. When we pore over various elements of psychoanalysis today—searching out the base elements of this school of thought—we see that it is basically reductionistic, limited by its own boundaries as to what it validates as real. Hence it will reduce any divergent theories to fit within its own framework. Therefore, as we expand beyond it, anything that goes beyond established limits as to who we are will be labeled wrong, dangerous, or untrue. This way of thinking maintains that we need experts to fix us when we're "broken," because we're like mechanical instruments incapable of helping ourselves. Freud's theories, understandably, were based on the physics of his time.

The gold that remains from this dross is the gift of psychoanalysis, reminding us of the crucial importance of making our unconscious motivations conscious to understand our behavior and the deep forces that move us. These wild and crazy instinctual "primary processes" residing within our unconscious minds also happen to be the creative force and primordial spirit that connects us to our earthly nature, keeping us alive—our dynamism.

The Contributions of Jung and Archetypal Psychology

While giving us a basis for deep self-exploration, Freud's view contained a flaw later examined by Dr. Carl Jung. Jung, often said to be Freud's most highly evolved student, later corrected Freud's limited approach to our unconscious mind. He observed from his experience that the "personal" unconscious was only *the superficial layer of the unconscious mind, resting upon a much deeper strata of the collective unconscious of the experience of all humanity.* His theory was that this greater unconscious mind was inborn, a universal unconscious mind he labeled "collective." The contents and patterns of behavior in this collective mind are basically the same for all people. They form a common psychic sub-strata, including our mythical and symbolic/archetypal realities: gods, goddesses, archetypal processes we undergo as evolving humans, and even our God-nature. Jung's view of the unconscious gave us a potential future and higher self, and not just a flawed past or inferior one. Jung's theory of the collective unconscious mind views us as proactive, not merely reactive, giving us a way to identify with images and archetypes that are greater than our egos.

Carl Jung developed a direct experiential understanding that our psyches are numinous (awesome, godlike, sacred, and mysterious). From his own deep inner explorations and spontaneous mystical experiences since childhood, Jung knew that "we are more than what we look like." He learned that, when accessed, our mystical subjective life matter-of-

74

factly shows evidence that our psyche, which is both our conscious and unconscious mind, is a spiritual entity, capable of intuitive wisdom, inspiration, and creativity that can have powerful life-changing effects upon us.

The word *psyche*, as I've said, means "soul" and is the root of the word *psychology*. Jung knew that our very soul should be the unit of analysis for the understanding of human nature. He knew that our soul, which is formless, uses the psyche as its reflective "partner" so it can experience itself in human form. He knew our psyche is vast, our total Self. Jung, in fact, participated in the beginnings of Alcoholics Anonymous, advising its founders that the alcoholic's craving was for spirit and that deep psychospiritual healing would be necessary to cure the plight of addiction. His famous phrase "spiritus contra spiritum" meant that it would take a spiritual approach to heal a spiritual illness. Jung also knew, however, that his discovery was ahead of its time, and that it might be generations before people could grasp the implication of this type of treatment for the suffering alcoholic.

The Archetypal Reality

Jungian dream work and the depth of inner work Jungian analysts facilitate have helped us recognize the archetypal dimension of our human and divine psyche. So inadvertently, Freud's attitude toward our unconscious mind may have stymied our growth (and may still) by stopping us short of enough curiosity or legitimate searching of our deep inner resources. He unintentionally built into us the fear of opening Pandora's box. For many of us today, this fear still guides us conveniently away from deep inner work, and consequently, the sacred creativity and revelations from the subjective side of life evade us as well.

Roberto Assagioli and Psychosynthesis

Another Freudian, Italian physician Roberto Assagioli, made a seminal contribution that sowed the seeds for a future spiritual psychology. He called his approach *Psychosynthesis*, a philosophy that validates both our human and spiritual natures. His definition of our psyche includes a fragmented ego nature, called "subpersonalities," and an integrator who lives "beyond ego," the transpersonal Higher Self.

The following story about Dr. Assagioli, which is remembered by his original students, will give you the flavor of the broad foundation he laid for us, and his basic difference with Freud.

At one point, shortly after the turn of the century, Sigmund Freud asked his student Roberto Assagioli to introduce Freudian analysis to Italy, to which Dr. Assagioli replied: (and I paraphrase) "Well, Dr. Freud, I will be happy to do this. However, you need to know that I would offer a few changes. Your model is like a house with a basement and a first floor, while my model of the psyche has a basement, a first, second, and third floor, a sun roof, and an elevator!" His work, by this very attitude, not only offers us a psychology of wholeness, but satisfies the soul! But it would be three quarters of a century before this highly sophisticated and well-developed theory of wholeness that includes all levels of human consciousness would take root and begin influencing the world.

In the meantime, mainstream human psychology, still seeking ways to determine and indeed, control the self, marched aggressively forward.

SECOND FORCE PSYCHOLOGY:

BEHAVIORISM AS A REACTION TO FREUD

As psychology advanced, behaviorism, or behavior modification, became the next evolutionary wave. The emphasis
was placed on technology and modifying human behavior
patterns through systematic reinforcement, positive or negative, to achieve desired behaviors. Humans were now able
to be quantified. By gradually learning new behaviors, using
techniques of experts, people were assumed to get happier.
This kind of help is beneficial for specific behaviors when
clear cause-and-effect is identified and concretely defined.

For example, if I fear heights because I barely survived a
plane crash, I can be desensitized into climbing back on a
plane and gradually learn to fly happily on my way. But if I
have anxieties that fall into some "existential" category
within my creative mind, such as vague feelings that my life
isn't working, that I am not a fit human being, or that I'm
about to be abandoned by the mate I love, then I'll drive my
poor behavioristic psychologist to utter distraction! He
won't be able to pinpoint what he is to modify. So his techniques will completely break down, which is often true of
machines!

For all its good points, behaviorism truly stripped away
our soul. Any idea of a metaphysical or "spiritual" nature
was not only unverifiable to the behaviorist, it was completely irrelevant. There was no legitimized way to believe
in a psyche or soul. The word *consciousness* did not reappear in the psychological worlds until the late sixties due to
this constricted perspective.

The behaviorists tried to correct each little symptom as
it came off the assembly line of habitual functioning. So

"symptom substitution" became a real problem during this phase of our psychological development. The personality tends to take on a new troublesome behavior to replace the one that got modified, the symptom that was blocked. Our psyche is too smart for this type of unrealistic approach to her healing. The human psyche has a way of finding a circuitous route to bring the symptom right back in our faces, to give us another chance to notice and release it. There will always be something new to paralyze us with fear once one phobia is cured, unless we've tapped into the depth of the issue and the Self is activated from within.

THE THIRD FORCE—HUMANISTIC PSYCHOLOGY:
THE "ME" GENERATION ENTERS THE SCENE

The Third Force in psychology, the humanistic era, came forth in the sixties as a reaction to the rigid robotism of behavior modification. These more broad-minded and easy-going humanists were lighter on the Self, having experienced more freedom from the controlling and creativity-blocking authority in their own lives. They wanted to expand the turf beyond reductionistic pigeonholes and diagnostic file cabinets of their predecessors, whom we now see only recognized the linear, analytical world of the intellect.

For the first time now, there was a respect for human feelings, attitudes, relationships, desire to be creative, intuition, and inner life where our real Self gives assent and volition to our choices. *Authenticity* became the key word for this school of thought. Now it became okay to just relax and be yourself, including even your angry, hurtful ego, if you were willing to claim your own needs and not push them off onto someone else in your life. This system of thought honored us for being just who we are in the truth of the moment.

In the encounter groups of this era, people would stay off your back as long as you were "being real." Going beyond the stimulus-response tape loop and stereotyped categories, the humanists helped people free up and see their beauty and uniqueness as individuals.

Humanistic psychology even validated going beyond "normalcy" as a sign of health, noting that people actually get bored with being "normal." When people's basic needs were met, it was discovered that they would become unhappy if they didn't move proactively toward goals and supernormal functioning. Phrases like "self-actualization," "peak experiences," and "ego transcendence" began to appear in the literature, and the expressions of our creativity and altruism were honored as higher needs.

Abraham Maslow's motivational theories and famous hierarchy of needs became widespread guidelines for growth, not only for people interested in psychology, but even for business and industry. Both our ego and our essence were now being observed and documented as the "becoming" and "Being" parts of our evolving self.

Encounter groups and sensitivity training popped up everywhere as weekend workshops and weekly retreats so that people could come together and express their truths to one another, hoping to receive validation and feedback from people they would mostly never see again, an experience that would give them more understanding of themselves and each other in their daily lives. Sometimes these groups were called "labs." We had definitely begun to experiment and widen our boundaries, especially in the areas of relationship and sexuality. More openness, more expression and experimentation were now accepted as healthy. Our creativity was freeing up—and so were our morals—which outraged the fundamentalist Christian segment of our society.

The humanistic movement was labeled the "Me" generation that heedlessly encouraged people to become self-serving with little sense of "otherness." People were accused of navel-gazing, becoming "workshop groupies," and losing a sense of service or the need to occasionally sacrifice for a loved one. And the "moral majority" of the late fifties and sixties labeled this work "secular humanism," its most fanatical members accusing it of being the work of the Antichrist.

Paradoxically, this ego-focused psychology taught us more about loving ourselves and forgiving others than had any of the previous schools. Third Force psychology planted the seeds for breaking up neurotic and codependent relationships by teaching us to stay in our own space and claim our feelings of the moment. This tracks parallel with the Twelve Step philosophy and programs where people listen in rapt attention to one another, one person at a time, and do not "take each other's inventory," staying respectful of fellow members as they share painful personal stories.

This era prepared us for legitimizing the unfolding of a potential self, rather than myopically focusing on ego repair. No longer were we just a singular body reacting to past conditioning. Our psychology had switched from reactive to proactive. Looking forward, rather than backward, toward an unfolding nature and goals for a more enlightened future, became legitimate for one's healthy motivation. Our wishes, hopes, dreams, and urges toward creativity could now enter the therapist's office without our being accused of escapism.

Because the humanists recognized that we have both lower (egoistic) and higher (meta) needs, which align more with our inner spiritual nature, they were the harbingers of Fourth Force psychology and religion that are now strengthening in the evolutionary march. The Self, on its journey toward wholeness, is now moving "beyond ego" and is searching for its sacred counterpart, the soul.

FOURTH FORCE PSYCHOLOGY:

WHEN SPIRIT COMES TO MIND

The spiritual psychologies include our divine reality and validate the inner subjective life and nonordinary states of consciousness. Through the work of transpersonal psychology, the various spiritual traditions, modern physics, and other fields of modern science investigating our depths, we are beginning to know better our essence, the Self.

The word *transpersonal* is an apt one for this movement; it means not only "going beyond the personal," but also "going through the personal." Pioneers in human research, such as psychologist William James and humanistic astrologist Dane Rudhyar, began to use this term back in the early 1900s. This relatively new field does not advocate bypassing personal inner work in the name of transcendence, but integrating our egos, *then* transcending them. There's a famous maxim from this school of thought: "You can't transcend an ego you've never had."

The concept for this new psychology came from great thinkers who realized that the higher, more essential core issues of human nature were being omitted from psychological thinking, This field stresses balanced development of the whole person, including physical, emotional, mental, and spiritual growth and transformation. The *being-level* of the person was recognized as who we are, not the knowledge and information-gathering levels of our ego's world. Both the inner and outer self, and the unconscious and conscious minds, are viewed as necessary for exploration, for complete human functioning.

The philosophical base for transpersonal psychology is derived from a merging of ancient wisdom and modern scientific findings. It legitimizes not only the human search for authenticity, but also for superconscious or transcendent ways of functioning. Transpersonal psychology's original statement of purpose noted a need for research and theory pertaining to human processes beyond, but including the personal values and states of consciousness such as unitive experiences, meta-needs, peak experiences, ecstasy, mystical experiences, bliss, self-transcendence, spirit, sacredness of everyday life, cosmic awareness, synergy, spiritual paths, psi phenomena, the value of working in altered states like meditation, and compassion. The spiritual dimensions of a person's functioning are acknowledged and provided the same credence as the ego and its trek through integrative functions. (*Journal of Transpersonal Psychology* 1969)

All types of spiritual psychology include the heart as a legitimate level of consciousness on its own—a bridge between our higher and lower functions. These holistic approaches move beyond the confines of psychology itself and take into account other fields of study, to give human creativity a fuller expression. They honor as healthy, not psychotic, our visions, dreams, and contacts with other sources with the Self that are viewed as mystical, supernormal, or even extraterrestrial, such as animal or spirit guides, inner teachers, masters, and entities from other dimensions who speak to us from within. Through researchers of human consciousness such as David Bohm, Karl Pribrim, Charles Tart, Kenneth Ring, Jean Achterberg, Stanislav Grof, Arthur Hastings, Michael Talbot, Rupert Sheldrake, Keith Thompson, Larry Dossey, Jean Houston, Robert Masters, Gay and Kathleen Hendricks, Ralph Metzner, Michael Harner, and Fred Alan Wolf, just to call out a few, the super-conscious mind has now donned its empirical face and become the subject in clinical research and the experimental laboratories of science.

The school of Jungian psychoanalytical and archetypal psychology is also blossoming today. Through the profound analysis of case studies in the work of Carl Jung and some of the finest scholarly Jungian therapists, such as Marie-Louise von Franz, Jolande Jacobi, June Singer, Robert Moore, Robert Johnson, Jean Shinoda Bolen, Marion Woodman, James Hillman, Clarissa Pinkola Estés, and others, we are finding out that our dreams and inner work contain the keys to our process of individuation. They guide us toward our highest, most actualizing goals.

These more expanded views of psychology that include the sacred were created by scholars of life who had had inner direct experiences that taught them we are "more than what we look like." These views were born of minds that lend authenticity of experience, people who had undergone nonordinary states of consciousness themselves and chronicled these inner journeys into the far reaches of human consciousness. Through their efforts, we are now beginning to see that it's not just a fantasy that we are capable of transcending time and space. Our multidimensional Self, who thrives on living in nonordinary states of consciousness, has become a solid fact in the concrete world of experimental science!

Through Eastern meditational approaches, spiritual disciplines, Jungian dream work, psychedelic research, near-death experiences, shamanic journeys, or other types of spontaneous mystical awareness, these founders no longer merely believed in a Soul or Higher Self; they *knew* these levels of conscious identity for themselves. And today there is ongoing research into death and dying, extrasensory perception, psychic healing, past-life recall, holographic brain physiology, quantum physics, and altered states catalyzed by psychedelics, posttraumatic stress, psychotic episodes, or varying forms of deep trance and meditation. We now hear of kundalini awakenings, the shamanic journey, psychic openings, or identifying with central archetypes as being valid experiences that can produce either a spiritual emergence (a breakthrough) or a spiritual emergency (a breakdown), which can lead to a profound "bottoming out" experience and subsequent transcendental rebirth, if dealt with therapeutically.

These new scientists can be recognized and appreciated for their pioneering efforts in areas that have not been popular to explore. They are risk-takers who have given us knowledge of the gift of wholeness in their willingness to risk their professional reputations on questions such as, Is there someone within our self that is larger than the ego? Can we get beyond our own ego mind to study it objectively? Is it legitimate to use divine or transcendent realities within the psyche and identify with these superhuman qualities? Do psyche and matter live together in one field within our human consciousness? In other words, can we study human consciousness in its entirety without becoming ego-bound once more, or even worse, filled with egoistic aggrandizement, dressed in white robes and speaking in the tongues of dead masters? These questions are being legitimately raised, and we hope our future will contain the answers as we continue to unfold the mystery of existence.

—

"Our Current Crisis Is a Personal and Planetary Birth" And It's Happening All At Once!

This statement came from my friend and colleague Barbara Marx Hubbard, and tracks perfectly with the findings of Eupsychia, our transformational healing and training program that's been in operation for twenty years. We're making a shift *away from neurotic-based theories of the self toward an understanding that we are birthing a new consciousness.* The former blocks the creative process and limits us through narrow diagnoses, while the latter understands and encourages the natural and chaotic ways of birth, seeing all its stages as natural and, in fact, fairly predictable—though everyone experiences birth uniquely. Viewing our symptoms of discomfort as those of a birthing defines us broadly as spiritual beings involved in an evolutionary process. This transpersonal Self-definition is empowering in itself.

Choosing to be *conscious* cooperators with the process of evolution is a brand new state of consciousness for us to embody on this Earth. It is an accelerated process that only happens in history at times like this, when a great cycle ends and some new type of species is being conceived. We've done this before, when the Christ manifested through Jesus. The Gnostic Christians held a belief that explained this "overlap" of two identities. They taught that the Christ was Jesus' "twin angel" who "descended from the heaven world and joined his earthly counterpart in an act of abiding union" (Hoeller 1992). This overshadowing by the archetypal Christ occurred during his baptism by John the Baptist, to bring about the cosmic event that Jesus was to manifest for the world.

Most of us still do not understand what happens when God and His creatures decide to evolve simultaneously. Two dimensions of consciousness activate at once, and we "all" go through it together. The Christ is a present and numinous factor in the psyche of humankind; the Christ-Image is a symbol for the whole and transpersonal Self. The Christ archetype is "a mediator" between Spirit and Matter, representative of the One Soul of Humanity.

An archetype such as the Christ can behave as a vicarious symbol of the individuation process, and we can give our power over to this divine Being in an act of faith. Or we can use this myth as a metaphor for the process of birthing a new consciousness and use Christ's story as our own guide to the personal experience of this cosmic process. Then we become fascinated by studying the significance of the various phases of Christ's life to better understand our own experience.

The first group, which does this by faith, becomes the fundamentalist branch of religion that rigidly upholds Jesus as "the only Son of God," a static icon we have no right to ever attempt to measure up to. This group calls it sacrilege if any one of us feels that we, too, must make this same journey for ourselves, interpreting Jesus's statements, "Do as I do," and "Follow me," and "Ye shall do greater things than I" as signs that he understood the process of evolution.

The second group, the "direct experiencers," does this process as metaphor. In the past they have been labeled heretic for their insistence that we all must become individuated souls. They see Jesus as an Elder Brother and model of a World Savior who "went first" to show us the way, and who is not frozen in time but is a fluid and dynamic soul, evolving as are we. (For a deeper understanding of this second approach, see Hoeller 1992.)

Jesus modeled for us beautifully how to take the qualities of the archetype, yet not become identified as it. He was a channel for the Messiah: Having touched this place within the psyche, he could therefore arouse wholeness in others who projected it onto him. Remember, He would say, "Who do you say that I am?" rather than walking in a state of aggrandizement.

All major religions have had their avatars or world saviors who function psychically for their followers in this manner. I focus on the Christ archetype because this is the one with which I am the most knowledgeable.

Self-empowerment is the key for the coming times we are already beginning to envision. A return of our own creativity is the key to the salvation of our planet and all her peoples! And it is certainly the cure for living neurotically, or lost in addiction and codependence! All naiveté and unexamined allegiance to authority are giving way now to an emerging New Order, which is based on the inner quest to find our own experience of truth. The release of our soul powers, the qualities of our real selves, is what frees up our "vision-making" faculties and can create new life.

WHERE WE CURRENTLY STAND

Today, we stand on the brink of our own future, feeling our way across a chasm of the unknown into the Aquarian Age. The symbol for this androgynous archetype, Aquarius, is the Water Bearer, who carries an urn on His/Her shoulders, sprinkling the world with "the waters of Life" whenever an arid climate or a dry patch is encountered on our dying terrain.

As we come through our changes, we must be careful not to become zealots and fall into the old trap of trying to force-feed our ways into others' minds, or to presume that we've found "the answer." We are simply to focus on our own continual healing and be willing to share our stories and inspiration with others who are hungry and are seeking our input.

Your task, when called out, is to activate the creative process by your own ability to be inspired. Your job is to awaken the hearts and enliven the minds of those now ready to transform. Inspiration is contagious! And you are all co-creators.

For creativity is not limited to those who stand out with a highly developed talent or skill; creativity is a matter of expression from one's own heart. It is a generic quality, our birthright, which affects anything that we touch with our own unique stamp of personal expression. We can be creative while unpacking a sack of groceries or paying our monthly bills. All our activities become creative when we are in love with every passing moment of our lives.

To become creative again, however, we must turn within. We must rediscover the psychic facts that are determining our true Reality and identities as co-creators. And all our instructions for this change we're undergoing are going to come from within—and not outside of us in any form of "Cosmic Enabler" who will "save us" from our own irresponsibilities!

The shift from outer to inner focus, and really placing your attention there, is how you will all get your instructions for your incoming Life. There is no other option. If it is already in existence, it is not new— and therefore not creative. The "new" must be a new conception. This is why all transformation must begin in the mind.

But this is a tall order, for modern people to learn to accept the truth of the inner life. Jung, the "master of the inner life," who focused more on the psychic worlds than any of psychology's ancestral chain, felt that our mania for physical explanations for everything is rooted in our fear of the metaphysical, for the two are "hostile brothers." Hence, anything unexpected that we cannot explain approaches us from the dark realm, we say. The unexplainable is regarded as dangerous, coming from an outside force and therefore real, or a hallucination, and therefore not true. "The idea that anything could be real or true which does not come from outside has hardly begun to dawn on contemporary man," Dr. Jung once lamented (1970, Vol. 10: 185).

PSYCHIC FACTS ARE REAL!

Psychic facts are those little pieces of *felt experiential data* that come in from your psyche's inner life. Though objective science may not always agree, *psychic facts are real.* They are just as "factual" as anything empirical or concrete could ever be—if not more so—for they actually affect our consciousness, causing our feelings, attitudes, or beliefs to change. In other words, they really happen, making us more open and aligned with our inner and true nature. When we begin to focus more on this inner life *which tends to cluster into meaningful events of soul activity and creative expression,* our attention starts to shift from outward focused information-gathering to the wisdom of the larger, more holistic inner Self.

Today we are setting the stage for the inner life as a dominant force in our transformation. This is the great shift modern psychology and psychotherapy are making. The shift to the importance of the inner life will balance out our currently lopsided nature and lead us toward wholeness. We are leaving the neurotic-based world and beginning to reframe our problems as the pangs of birthing a new consciousness. This shift is the philosophical underpinning for every word in this book. We set the stage, remain harmless and loving, and Spirit will do the rest. This faith in Spirit is no longer mere wishful thinking; it is a tried and true conviction.

Chapter Six

PREPARING FOR THE LIFE OF SPIRIT

[People] are used to thinking that anything higher than they has to be divine beings—that is, without a body— who appear in a burst of light.... But it isn't like that at all...a new mind is being formed. And the body is learning its lessons. All bodies, all bodies.
—*Satprem*, The Mind of the Cells

Though many of us intellectually agree, we've not fully awakened to the implications of our spiritual identity *as fact.* The recognition of our inherent spiritual nature has not yet had the psychological or cultural impact on us that it eventually will. We make our life choices and behave as though we are only egos. We are trapped in our intellects and story lines from the past, and they are rapidly becoming too small to contain us. As planetary citizens on the brink of disaster, we are charged now with the awesome responsibility of seeing it all, and ourselves, quite differently.

Before we can begin to think of being whole, we must merge our two identities consciously, our ego's and our soul's. Both these natures need to be recognized and served, and then they can unite as One. We must learn to respect the dualism we've been trapped in for so long. Then we can learn to live as an *antinomy*, being *both* human *and* divine, rather than either/or.

The marriage of ego and soul is an evolutionary stage we encounter at some point on our journey of completion. This merger is the highest union possible while we exist in human form. It is embodying spirit, uniting spirit and matter, dissolving all duality—at long last! It is an "alchemical" process that happens inwardly and energetically, a literal transmutation that affects every aspect of our nature. This sacred marriage brings us a whole new identity: a Self who no longer takes it so personally. A concretized incarnated ego blends with soul essence, becoming light-hearted and full of good will.

For this new Self to manifest in our ordinary lives, however, we must learn how to *do* this new identity by actually *being* it, by taking on its ways of synthesis, high-mindedness, and love. Our bodies will naturally become more youthful and jubilant, the same way we feel when we have fallen in love. We will become filled with compassion, in blissful yearning and anticipation for fulfillment of this love. Our minds will begin to settle, and we will no longer be distracted from our real inner work, that of becoming whole.

Our addictions and attachments to outer conditions have been in the way of this loving and more integrated way of being complete within ourselves. Attachments to our past storylines and certain people we thought we couldn't live without kept us focused in the wrong direction, as we sought to ease our spiritual hunger through unhealthy dependent ways.

Searching for things outside ourselves to complete us blocks our connection to the inner life and our true identities. I cannot emphasize this enough. This outer focus is responsible for losing our Self-empowerment as we live through the "wilderness experience" told of in so many myths. We wander aimlessly through outer conditions, looking for our real life. And slowly, it dawns on us (through many disappointments and blind alleys!) that our private, subjective experiences in the inner life inform us of the ways of Spirit.

As you read, you will be reminded about wisdom you already possess but perhaps lost touch with along your way. And though you may not yet realize what all this means to you, you will read some things that will anchor this holistic truth. Then, in your own way, you will realign with a stronger and more vital sense of your Self.

THE IMPORTANCE OF INNER WORK

There is a price to pay for taking this ride that consciously brings our divinity into human form. Our soul must sacrifice the right to remain unruffled in the flowing, unimpeded spiritual realities and be tossed instead into the intense involvement of existence, unanesthetized! Totally present in our bodies, as separate "particles" in this space/time continuum, we are required to involve in the abundant but challenging and dualistic human condition— with passion and full intention! This is the requirement of merging the ego with the soul.

The human psyche was designed to work out, or *live through*, the trials and tribulations of full realization. Through this paradoxical process we become unique expressions of the one divine Self here on Earth. To accomplish this, we're required to make every aspect of the unconscious mind fully conscious in our ordinary world of everyday events. And some things rise up and integrate quite easily, while others can create much havoc in our lives.

⌒

THE SCIENCE OF THE SOUL

This work of individuation, as you may suspect, is no small feat: To make it through this "sacred ordeal," we must shift from dependency on externally focused empirical science and worldly authority, to the inward way of *psychic fact*. For it is through our private subjective dreams, visions, and inner longings that the soul's intentions can be accessed.

So, what exactly is a *psychic* fact, or the science of the soul? Well, it's anything that brings an *emotional* or *numinous* effect upon one's consciousness in such a way that a *felt shift* occurs and brings about some new result. You valued a certain thing, or held some great opinion, and now, because of some numinous inner experience and profound recognition, the whole scene changes and what you held dear no longer seems all that relevant. Some part of your past loses its hold on you. Through the science of the soul, we learn to see our outer life as the mirrored reflection of our soul's status in its descent into matter, and we stop taking the external life as the totality of our experience.

Jung said that our logic can overlook these inner truths, but can never really eliminate them, for they are the *real*-est thing about us. Later on, science may call this numinous inner life a great discovery, and someone will win the Nobel

Prize. For materialistic science will always eventually catch up with the mystics in legitimizing the spiritual life. But in truth, it should not matter one whit to us whether anyone else perceives our inner perceptions as truth. For we are each one our only meaning-makers! There is never a real external judge or absolute outer authority on you; this has all been a giant illusion. It's all inside.

The "new physics" already backs Jung's view by defining the enfolded (inner) and unfolded (outer) life as the same and of equal value. We now know that there's an elasticity to the "stuff" we're made of that keeps our essence from ever betraying itself into the confines of either/or. The simplest law of particle/wave theory states that the two modes of being are one; that the rational and nonrational coexist quite amicably, not jostling each other in their fluid, ever-changing inner world. Therefore, it is not at all unscientific of us to claim as valid what occurs in our inner life, though it is considered "subjective" and "nonrational." In fact, it is that essential "other" side of our nature that has not yet been explicated from the whole and made visible into discrete "particles" (or personalities). Brugh Joy's commanding, "The dark, the light, no difference!" affirms this Truth. And once this psychic fact sinks in, it even gets better: We recognize ourselves as creators right alongside God. We begin to see clearly that whatever we choose to give our full intention will manifest in the outer world.

To decode what the psyche experiences as scientific fact, however, requires a big commitment on our part. We have to develop our perception of the inner realms and truly understand the messages and images our dreams and imaginings bring us from the subjective life. It's not enough to merely wonder about this inner Reality-in-the-making, then casually watch it fade. We must be willing to interpret these dispatches from our soul, and draw conclusions about what our Self is trying to tell us.

With full intention we engage the content of our minds, even do a psychic inventory and classification if need be, and get at it all scientifically. Your own intention creates the science project. The formula: Set up the *experiment, experience* its ups and downs, and then serve as its *expression*; i.e., become a living piece of data representative of the archetypal ideal. This is the true science of soul-making, our only real task in life—and the only work that ever really makes us feel content. But we must remember: any lack or negligence concerning the recognition and willingness to examine these inner realizations can result in the same destructive effects that any sloppy research project will produce.

THE NATURE OF SPIRIT

This word *spirituality* has been so confused with the word *religion*, its working definition used in this book deserves a moment of our attention. For us, spirituality connotes "an inner refining process." We adopt physicist John Hitchcock's definition that our spirituality is "an internal shaping force" (1991). Our spirituality is an immaterial "sprightliness." When we are filled with spirit, we feel that God is living us and we are living God. Spirituality is not an outcome; it is a process, one of becoming more likened unto our inner God-Image. To use our consciousness to become Self-aware (soul-dominated) is what we mean by spirituality. For me, becoming conscious and becoming spiritual are synonymous terms. I've seen that our spiritual life enlarges as we move continually toward a newer and greater morality, taking hold of our process of evolution and participating consciously.

Spirituality is not about being religious. A religion is an *outer form* that our spiritual lives can take, where we identify with or are fascinated by the traditions or theological beliefs that belong to a particular culture or group. This is religion. The original meaning of the word *religion* was "to link back." Unfortunately, many religious people have lost this universal sense of the word and apply it only to their specific version of God and the nature of the universe.

People who seek spirituality through an inner pathway become *knowers*. This is what the word *gnostic* means, "the desire to know." People who seek spirituality in the outer world become theologians; they are *believers*. The latter often study *about* spirituality, but they may not have direct experiences with it. God is a concept to contemplate or study, not necessarily to experience. During an interview Carl Jung was asked: "Dr. Jung, do you believe in God?" And he answered, "No, I don't believe in God; I *know* God."

When people begin making the shift from *believing*, based on others' doctrines, to *knowing*, based on personal numinous inner spiritual experience, they often do not know if it is safe to speak out loud about this. I hear people say they are metaphysical and pursue the inner path secretly, because they fear negative labels for having an interest in these matters—even in the 1990s! And, unfortunately, it is true that we need to protect ourselves from these blasts. There are indeed people today who adhere to rigid beliefs and label all inner searching to be "of the devil."

Great religious scholars such as Tielhard de Chardin,

Meister Eckhart, and recently, former Dominican priest Matthew Fox, have been excommunicated and silenced for bringing knowledge of the path of direct experience to others. Yet all scriptures lead to this, when they are interpreted beyond the programming of fear-based religions. For instance, as I mentioned earlier, in the Holy Bible, Jesus said to his disciples, "Ye shall do greater things than I." And St. Paul said that it is through the transformed mind that we will find spirit. Revelations states: "We shall all be changed in the twinkling of an eye."

Many references to transformation and the "kingdom of God within" appear in the Bible. Yet other more fixed beliefs state that Jesus is cast in stone, static, and will never evolve. Some people even believe that the word *evolution* is un-Christian. Yet Christ told us over and over that we should walk the Way of the Christ, to unfold our own divinity as He modeled for us. So it would seem that it is biblical to say that we are all sons and daughters of God, and that we each have "our part" to do by becoming fully aware of our divinity while we are here in human form. Many original Christians held this sanctification of humanity as "a knowing."

We've got to do some work to catch up to what the Self already knows about our nature. To begin, try to intuit the difference between being spiritual and being religious. If you will put this out to your Higher Self, you will begin to receive your answers about this important subject from the God-within.

＞

The Ego Is Concretized Spirit

We grow an ego up from the Earth, once it is birthed through a mother's body. And once the ego matures, we embody Spirit "from the top, down" as it descends to reclaim its earthly counterpart. The ego must become permeable so that Spirit can enter. Psyche, our incarnated soul, makes this permeability possible. She enters into our ordinary lives with her qualities of compassion, spontaneous delight, and a magical curiosity that can transform anything she interacts with into love and light. Until the concretized ego and the fluid soul can blend in this sacred act of "holy matrimony," known as the *hierosgamos* of the alchemists, we are trapped in the dualism of warring opposites of egoism and a soulful life.

The *ego* is the executor of our personality, as noted by the great psychiatrist, Sigmund Freud. But the ego isn't "a thing"; we can't open ourselves up and find one living in our bodies. It is a psychic construct, an *archetype* we acknowledge as real, one that sits at the boundary between the unconscious and conscious mind. It is a gatekeeper, deciding what to allow into our consciousness as "reality" and what to close off or reject. When it rejects something, it's as though that thing does not exist. The ego builds a psychological defense structure called "denial" that won't let us recognize that which is too painful or perceived as too dangerous to give credence to.

The ego's function is to keep us focused on the personal life long enough to integrate our physical, emotional, and mental "bodies" in a manner that society will accept. In this way, we can become functional within our culture and can later serve it, when we become wise from our experiences. The ego is therefore invested in looking good, in either fitting into the group or in standing out as a popular and successful idiosyncratic personality. The ego seeks pleasure and gratification of all its needs, and it thrives on being right.

Certain spiritual paths, both Eastern and Western, teach that the ego is pure illusion, or that we are to "kill off desire." These may be scholarly high truths that ring of authenticity in the abstract realms of spirit. But I believe these are confusing mandates for the unsophisticated thinker. While here in this ordinary world where most of us live in a body, these teachings can become serious stumbling blocks to our process of becoming whole: They are absorbed and misinterpreted as despising our humanness, a "splitting off" that leads us down a primrose path into a spiritual bypass.

I know what these teachers are attempting to imply: that we must watch out for an unredeemed ego filled with self-destructive drives who can cause ourselves and others harm. And because we live on a planet where there is free will, it's true that a shadowy, unconscious ego can break off from Spirit and run amuck. We all know how it feels to be in the presence of egotism.

But the question is: How do we deal effectively with this *fact* of our being, this ego we inhabit? The lighted way reveals a nondualistic approach to this issue that will keep us on the mark, moving us toward unification of the opposites: In your mind's eye, envision Spirit as abstract "vapor." And the soul, as it moves on down toward materialization can be viewed as "water." Then envision the ego as "ice." Though each form changes at the varying levels of consciousness—spirit, soul, matter—the essence remains the same. This will give you a more workable picture to hold in your mind as you explore this issue for yourself.

The ego, then, is our "concretized" soul, our psyche's outer expression, designed to protect the personal identity; it is not meant to be universal or cosmic. It is purely "personalistic"—and dualistic—valuing everything in terms of comparison, either wrong or right. For this is its essence, its sacred purpose. And though given bad press with negative labels like egotistical, separatist, or narcissistic, the ego is our best friend. A healthy ego discriminates between what we can and can't handle, so our ego protects us from unwelcome intrusions from others, even from our own unconscious. It can keep us from becoming overwhelmed with stress, or even psychotic, by making our bodies sick, repressing our feelings, or acting out. By filling us with fear or by labelling something unreal or dangerous, our ego assures that we'll stay away from it.

When we have enough ego strength to handle something new, the ego lets up a little and allows us to take it in. Once the ego feels that we've become strong, emotionally balanced, and possessors of a realistic and positive self-image, it relaxes its hold on us and looks toward the soul, or Higher Self, for a new task. Its job will now be to bring knowledge of the material world to the spiritual Self, its Divine Partner, our soul. Our ego's highest function is to materialize spirit. The ego hungers for the higher life, and once gratified in the concrete world, it seeks to align with its higher needs, the yearning to transcend its nature—to be creative, loving, and high-minded.

THE "STUFF" THAT SOULS ARE MADE OF

The soul is not a "thing" but a set of qualities representative of Spirit. It is a transitional entity, only needed to blend our spiritual and material (ego) selves. It is the mediator between Spirit and matter. The soul cannot truly be defined, but it can be known as a metaphor, some of the more common being the Christ Consciousness, the Indwelling Flame, the Higher Self, the Solar Angel, the Observer or Onlooker, and our Individuality. We think of the soul as the essence of a thing, the conscious factor in all forms.

The soul's qualities are those of spontaneity, joy, serenity (bliss), creative imagining, inspiration, intuition (a felt sense of truth), deeply held compassion for others, playfulness, harmlessness, loving-kindness, and childlike curiosity. The soul's true desire is to serve humanity, but it delights in the sensual pleasures as well. It knows that we are immortal, and it is not afraid of death.

The soul is attracted to the ego as "the experiencer self." It hungers for the pleasures of the earthly life, and goes about involving in these pleasures through merging into the ego's concrete ways, bringing with it the ways of Spirit.

—

THE EGO AND THE SOUL MUST COME INTO RIGHT RELATIONSHIP

The ego and soul are an *antinomy*—paired opposites existing side by side within the totality of the whole. They represent an "oppositeness" that can never be combined or each would lose its true and unique gift of expression. Each completes the other through a paradox: blending into a oneness where each retains its distinctive nature.

The ego goes through developmental stages of becoming strong, effective in the outer world, and assured that it knows how to "gatekeep" for its host. Once the ego is established as a stable server of our personality, it is drawn upward toward a higher way of helping us. It turns toward the soul. Then it slowly sacrifices its dominance in our lives, which we experience as ego death. As it turns toward the act of surrender, which doesn't come naturally, the ego comes into its right relationship to the soul. Now the ego can teach the soul of the Earth's ways and is a receptor of soul qualities from "on high."

The soul must, in return, come into right relationship with the ego, for it is totally incompatible with egoistic ways. The soul carries with it a deep sense of love and respect for the qualities of the ego, those strengths and abilities to manage and concretize things of the material world. The soul dissolves into the ego, leading it lovingly into surrender. As the ego's hardened edges melt away, the personality is permeated with the soul's light—qualities of spontaneity, light-heartedness, inspiration, childlike curiosity, and creative imagining.

Stop a minute right now and remember the last time you felt this way. You can always tell when your soul has overtaken your ego's dominance over your nature, for you become less intense, less invested in outcomes, and more willing to just relax into the moment. Your sense of humor returns, and you are open-hearted and easy to be with. Often, spurts of joy are the result. Even when your life contains harsh realities you cannot currently get past, you will feel moments of actual bliss that "come upon you like fate" while merely driving down the street, or in the middle of grocery shopping. And gradually, you begin to feel the bliss that is your heart's true essence, and you can anchor this feeling and even invoke it consciously from time to time.

So you see, both the ego and the soul must undergo sacrifice to become one Self. But let's remember that the word *sacrifice* means "to make holy." It is not the awful thing we've made it out to be from our ego's point of view. As our soul-consciousness enters into our awareness, the ego loses its hardened opinions and begins to feel less in charge. This is terribly frightening at first and causes many a person to bolt, or to become more rigid for a while. Eventually, as the Great Work proceeds within us, the soul melts down, giving up its definition, indeed, its very life, to be absorbed into our personalities.

This is the work of Self-creation. Through the willingness to consciously merge the ego and the soul, we will have created a vehicle that is ready and willing to manifest Spirit on Earth. The transpersonal Self can walk into our bodies, our hearts, and our minds.

Soul-Work	Ego-Work
(activates from the top down)	(activates from the bottom up)
Responds	Abstracts and Ascends
Descends	Death/Rebirth ("cooks," transforms)
Dissolves Substance in the "waters" (makes pliable)	Surrenders
Extracts "the Gold" (molds, sculpts into Ideal)	Invokes
Embodies	Looks Upward

In metaphysics, it is understood that we undergo this stage in our evolution where the soul disappears, having released all its qualities into our concretized nature, becoming now the Self (a materialized entity who can exist in the world of form). And the soul is no longer a mediator between spirit and matter. It has given us its life. Now, we are a being in the world who "goes to the Father," as Jesus did. We are in touch with Spirit directly through our bodies.

Or, again, in classical metaphysics, the Monad (we, as individualized "sparks of the God-force") are communicating directly with our physical bodies. Spirit and matter have merged. This is the culmination of the journey of awakening to our true identities as spirit in form.

INNER WORK IS THE WAY THROUGH

Inner work is the key to our transformation, especially during this time of planetary crisis. For we are being prepared to usher in a new state of consciousness for this planet, and the information is coming in, not from space brothers or a messiah landing on a mountain top and saving us from our woes; it's coming in through our unconscious minds, through us. Personal and planetary transformation is an inside job that may indeed manifest outwardly, when the inner brings it forth. It's up to us.

The process of psychospiritual integration is learned from a willingness to experience "inner work." Through a recognition of both the *symptoms* in our outer life and the *symbolic* processes unfolding from within, this process accesses both our psychological and our spiritual nature. Most people are more familiar with the ways of psychology and less familiar with the ways of spirit. For it is through the less-known processes that access the collective unconscious mind from within, including the Mind of our Creator-God, that we open to direct spiritual experiences. We learn to recognize these numinous processes as "legitimate" and essential to our healing. Here, we are running ahead of hard-core scientific psychology (as mystics are prone to do!).

It is a fact that our obsessive outer focus on the past—

our addictions, attachments, and limited storylines—are holding us back from recognizing our true gifts and spiritual inheritance. But we tend to remain stuck in our past until we can fully heal and understand what we have been through. Therefore, all work of a psychospiritual nature will begin with "shadow work" and regression back into our past to heal, accept, and forgive any aspects of our experience where we've taken on wounding and limitation. *To heal* means "to make whole" (holy), and wholeness has no missing parts. Often, this work includes a reexamination of old taken-for-granted beliefs that have come from our family traditions, religious training, and other orthodoxies.

We must all come through psychological healing if we are to be an undistorted representative of Spirit here. We must never become arrogant, or products of a "spiritual bypass," for Spirit has to come through the human psyche to manifest in this world. Consequently, a spirituality without a cleared out psyche is going to be a spirituality fraught with the distortions of that particular psyche/soma vehicle. There is no way around this fact as long as we are dwelling within a body/ego/brain.

To be true spiritual warriors at this turning of the evolutionary wheel, we must all come out of denial concerning any of our lopsided parts. We'll be required to make conscious our own descent into "the underworlds" of egoistic separatism, selfishness, and ignorance. Our soul, who, through innocence, has gotten trapped in matter, needs retrieval. The only way to save this world is through clearing out the human psyche of all its clutter and unconscious ways. Then we will be able to visit the "heaven worlds" anytime we wish, without distorting this higher spiritual reality with our own egoistic desires. In this way, we can function on any level of Reality by our invocation and commitment to Spirit. So we can all return to Love. But this work is hard to do without building a good bridge between the lower and higher worlds.

"And Help Me to Do 'My Part'"

As this century, and indeed an entire Age in human history, comes to a close, we must learn to let evolution do us, rather than trying so hard to do it. The ego simply cannot "cap it off" and decide which set of conditions it must go to next; it doesn't have that power. So many of us are currently undergoing "the renunciation initiation" as the ego relinquishes its dominance over the personality, with a new-found willingness to own none of it, yet remain steadily responsible for (and respondable to) a higher order.

In our Eupsychia intensives, we use an invocation in a ceremonial manner: *For so it must be! And help me to do "my part!"* You will recognize "your part" by your fascination with certain challenges in life and specific aspects of "the new." Our dreams and visions will relentlessly out-picture what we are in the process of making happen, for the inner life has quickened and is rising up to show us the way. To summarize, then, the *modus operandi* for "our part" in this divine world drama is this:

1. *Focus our intention*
2. *Align with the energy of our Higher Power*
3. *Surrender consciously to the archetypes that move us*
4. *Continually practice being "in the Presence" of that inner One whom we've learned to trust as God*

It's up to us now to invoke these changes and make them real by feeling our way into the new life that's pouring in and learning to *be* it. Carl Jung knew of these worlds, and his works can help guide us through these "threshold times." Our process can be smoother from the sheer understanding of it. As the meaning-makers, what we must do is validate the archetypal inner kingdom as real—accept it as *fact*—then these divine universal processes can do the work of transformation through us. Whenever the entire human race enters into a transformational cycle, such as this current turn of the wheel, the archetypal dimension moves in, overshadowing our little ego's limited ways. Archetypes carry the designs for the newly emerging Self. They are our own Ideals! These are our "architects of Being."

Chapter Seven

ACCESSING THE FUTURE: THE WORLD OF THE ARCHETYPES

If one knows that one has been singled out by divine choice and intention from the beginning of the world, then one feels lifted beyond the transitoriness and meaninglessness of ordinary human existence, and transported to a new state of dignity and importance, like one who has a part in the divine world drama.

—*Carl Jung*, Answer to Job

PLAYERS IN THE "DIVINE WORLD DRAMA"

We've seen now that when the ego and the soul unite, our human psychology begins to formulate the ways of abstract spirit. With this bridge between these two dimensions of consciousness, we can now engage our minds with our Higher Power's sacred functions. We can literally begin to "see" with our inner eye how our Higher Power works. And what a fascinating world this is! It is filled with symbols of the universal ways *all* human beings act and feel, archetypes that are built into our psyche. Archetypes act on us beyond the conscious control of our ego, influencing our lives. Because they are God's "hands and feet," they are also divine. Through their influences on our psychic life, they shape-shift us into better people as we trek through phases of Becoming.

Before Jung's time, Sigmund Freud had given us only a superficial understanding of our unconscious mind, reducing it to a storage place for all our repressed personal psychological baggage. We had to be in analysis forever to understand the unconscious motivations that were ruining our lives. Jung found, however, that the unconscious mind is much greater than Freud had realized, capable of accessing all of human memory—even humanity's future. He determined that the mind matrix (psyche) contains all human possibilities, past, present, and future—the archetypes in the collective unconscious. John Hitchcock agrees:

> It is easily and clearly seen that the unconscious must contain all future human and posthuman potentials, just as the human is the potential of the unconscious hydrogen of the early cosmos. (1991: 22)

Freud may have influenced your thinking more than you realize. And you, too, may have a limited and unexamined view of the power of your unconscious mind. You may believe that all your unconscious motivations and behaviors stem from the repressed biographical "stuff" of your personal life that hasn't been assimilated and healed, and that this is what makes you dysfunctional or neurotic, full of complexes and such. Well, yes. There may indeed be some parts of you that still are not healed from your past, and these issues do exist in your personal subconscious mind—

parts of your shadow self. In a later section of the book, we'll take some time to deal with this superficial layer of your unconscious mind. But listen carefully: *You are more than this!*

THE PERSONAL AND THE COLLECTIVE UNCONSCIOUS MIND

Jung saw a personal definition of the unconscious as only a superficial layer of the unconscious mind, however, and he coined the term *collective unconscious* for the greater part he felt Freud left out. Jung knew, from his own profound inner work and that of his patients—dream work, inner visions, and powerful artwork—and further, from his intensive study of human history, that we are tied to a much greater archaic collective unconscious mind that emits universal symbols and processes we all share. He believed that it isn't possible to separate ourselves from all that has affected us as a collective soul. Dr. Jung therefore has contributed to our knowledge of wholeness and expanded our consciousness by giving us both a personal and a collective psyche to work through and make conscious.

Archetypes are the *a priori* patterns of all possible creations that reside in the "tissues" of our psyche. They are the psyche's structure and are therefore *psychic facts*. And psychic facts, as I've said, are "real-er than real," for they impact our psyches dramatically and cause us to change. In other words, though they are energetic patterns we cannot see, they definitely exist. They represent the patterns of wholeness that God apparently thought of when He created us. Archetypes for humanity are all our possible patterns; they shape the evolution of our species.

All our human struggles and conditions are representative of aspects of the collective. We are here to take on the archetypal human situations—Birth, Death, Childhood, Marriage, Maturation, Transformation, and so on. And the archetypal personages—Mother, Father, Lover, Hero, Healer, Servant, and so on—as well. We are always taking on some part of an archetypal collective pattern that is of Humanity, of our One Body. And we must never forget this; otherwise, we get lost in our personal story lines, separating from our roots. Then we feel isolated and irrelevant in the grand scheme of things—which is *not* Reality. We are never "just" doing something personal or unique to us. This knowledge alone, if absorbed, is transformative; it will give you a sense of meaning and high purpose. So stop right now and really take this in, through a moment of deep Self-reflection.

When we touch into this dimension of our consciousness, all things humanly possible can be accessed. Then, if we will image (imagine) one of these possibilities, we can bring it down from the abstract into the concrete mind, and this potential can be ours. Spirit is materializing through us in this manner. Through our own creative mental intentions and abilities, we Self-create: *we are the reality-makers of our personal world.* Remember, in the new physics, we've learned that "the observer disturbs."

Archetypes are best understood as the organs in the psyche's "body." And just like our physical organs, each one has its particular function for our Higher Power to perform in our unfolding Self-creation. You could think of archetypes as God's Thoughts, which become our *Imago Deo* (our Images of God). I like that! Through the archetypal realm we directly connect with God's mind; it gives us the opportunity to picture our God-nature.

All human beings, being of one Soul called "Humanity," experience the very same archetypal patterns, or matrices, which are beyond form. However, the *images* of these patterns that we picture in our minds vary in form from culture to culture and with different cycles of time, depending on how a person or culture "sees" or imagines them. The universal ideal of the Warrior or Heroine would look quite different to an Italian than to an Asian. Your idea of the archetypal Lover, for instance, would not be dressed in the same costume or the same hair-do that you'd imagine if you had lived in the seventeenth century. But underlying all these cultural and societal differences, there is a universal constancy to the ideals we are attempting to express.

Philosophers will recognize the archetypal images as the world of Plato's Ideal. *Everything* has its archetypal original design. Otherwise, it could not be imagined and therefore not a candidate for creation. The perfect flower, the perfect house, the perfect love letter, the perfect marriage, the perfect birth, the perfect philosophy, and on and on, we would probably all agree that these are such Ideals. But we would probably *not* all agree on the form the "perfections" might take. At the level of the *archetypal image,* this is where our individual differences come into play. It is important to remember that theoretically there is a difference between an archetype (simply an abstract energy matrix) and the archetypal ideal (closer to manifestation and already "colored" by our experience and our ways of thinking).

The psyche is the soul's way of knowing itself as "something formulated"—the soul's beloved reflection. Psyche is our repository for all human nature and expression, both conscious and unconscious. The soul must come through the archetypal dimension on its descent into our concrete world and take on its "faces" and "costumes." Archetypes enable us to "see" our divinity so we can experience "the play of consciousness." But as part of our psychic life, and not our physical life, we also need to remember that an archetype never takes on concrete form in the outer world, but *formulates symbolically and affects us from within.* Or, if we cannot "read" its inner messages, it speaks to us through our dreams, visions, and intuitive revelations. We may draw a picture of our rendition of an archetype. Or describe it in a poem. Yet though we never meet an archetype while walking down the street, it *can and does* cause "symptoms" in our physical lives if we hit up against an archetypal pattern that's never been made conscious, which we call "a complex." So when we act out one of these divine impulses unconsciously, either positively or negatively, we are under the influence of an archetypal complex. Unconsciously, they can harm us; consciously, they enable us to grow.

So by now I hope you are getting the picture that the powerful archetypes, which have been following us since our inception as human beings, are a conglomerate of the Higher Self with all its universal human motifs. We all, as little individual selves, will pass through them to achieve a state of fulfillment, which will be filling in the Pattern that is our essence. The Self, of course, is the central archetypal Human, the One at the helm of all our activities of Self-creation. When we say "our center," "our core," or "our root-consciousness," we are talking about the archetypal and transpersonal Self "from whence we sprung." The Self can manifest as an archetypal

Person or a Process, symbolizing whatever transformative activity is currently "up" for any one of us at any given time during our process of individuation.

Some most commonly recognized archetypes that we encounter and integrate are the Infant, Child, Mother, Father, Maiden, Youth, the *Puella* or *Puer Aeternis* (Eternal Child), Lover, Husband, Wife, Shadow, Warrior, Messenger (Avatar), Server, Savior, Wise Old Woman, Wise Old Man, God/Goddess, King/Queen, Magician, Healer, Christ, Buddha. Representatives in our dream life and transpersonal visions for the archetypal Self are often Jesus as the Christ; Siddhartha Guatama as the Buddha; Sophia, Isis, or the Mother Mary as the Divine Feminine; and Shiva/Shakti, the Hindu God/Goddess. And we all are capable of accessing this Patterning—or any archetypal processes of these incarnated beings—as models for ascension of consciousness. You will probably recognize Birth, Loss of Innocence, Baptism, Transfiguration, Betrayal, Crucifixion, Resurrection (Transmutation), and Ascension as being "the Path of the Christ." Depending on where you are in your own awakening process (of remembering that you, too, are divine), you will undergo certain aspects of these Experiences. But remember, these are universal human psychospiritual experiences, which all of us are capable of accessing in the subjective life. No one ever has a corner on the market. This would be a form of psychosis called "becoming identified as a central archetype."

GOD-THINGS ALWAYS COME IN PAIRS

And there are many, many others, known by some form or another in every culture's roots. But they are not always as acceptable as Isis, the Christ, or the Buddha! These Divine Characters who emanate from this more holistic dimension can also be Super Negative and can wreak havoc on our lives, if allowed to run around in our psyche's mind unconsciously. We've all heard people say things like: "She's a 'Jezebel'; don't trust her." "This feels like Kali, the Goddess of Destruction." Or "The Devil made me do it." Or, "I'm going through a heavy betrayal, or loss." We'll hear from an astrologer that we're in a Saturn return, that Mercury is in retrograde, the Sun is on our horizon, or Jupiter is showering abundance on our professional life. We may comment that someone is being an egotistical Leo, a picky Virgo, or a typical Scorpio who "stings." The astrological signs and figures are archetypes that both positively and negatively affect our ways of being.

They all have their divine function to play in the activities of creation. If positive, they bring us to a new state of fulfillment; if negative, they bring us an important lesson, resulting, we hope, in a successful passage through some great Ordeal. And though some of them tear up our lives or cause us to act in ways that hurt before they transform, we discover more and more of their sacred purpose as we get to know them better. In fact, it's good to form a relationship with the ones you know are hanging around. Therefore, if we are desirous to live "the symbolic life" it's good to befriend the archetypes, and then hold steady when their energies overtake your smaller life. As long as you are willing to make the Unconscious conscious, it will never overwhelm you. So staying conscious through inner work is the key to our advancement as a human soul.

CARL JUNG'S SPECTRUM OF THE PSYCHE

The archetypes are the "instincts" of the psychic world, as earlier stated, built right into the fabric of our psyche's "body." Therefore, psyche and soma are interactive. An archetype is the "psychic feeling" and image we have about *the whole nature* of a thing. For instance, the essence of transformation is Death/Rebirth, and when active, will bring you through such a sequence in your life. The essence of Cupid/Eros is "falling in Love," so when this archetype pops into our lives, we fall head over heels for someone. Archetypes bring our essence, which is abstract, into unique psychic functions, so we can work from their patterns toward our wholeness. An understanding of this dimension of consciousness is essential to our fulfillment.

Just as we all know human *instincts* can seize us physically in ways we don't have conscious control over, *archetypes* grab us psychically with the same dramatic autonomy. Instincts are aspects of the *material* world, reactions to things like poisonous snakes or a tree about to fall on your head. They reside at the infrared end of the unconscious spectrum. When the instinct for physical survival crops up, for example, you respond instantly with an involuntary reaction that saves your physical life. Archetypes operate on us in the very same fashion, but they fall at the other end of the spectrum (at the ultraviolet end). Because archetypes are *psychic* in nature, and the dynamic that activates them is psychological (and not visible to us like snakes and trees are), our reactions to an archetypal stimulus don't always appear rational to ourselves or those who observe our behavior.

Let's look at all this graphically for a minute, the way Carl Jung did, so we can make this very plain. You can picture this like colors viewed through a prism, with physical instincts as being at one end of the continuum, in the invisible infrared spectrum, while the archetypes occur all the way at the other end, in the ultraviolet sphere:

Infrared, red, orange, yellow, green, blue, indigo, violet, ultraviolet

physical instincts	**psychic archetypes**
(hidden in the	*(hidden in the*
invisible worlds	*invisible worlds*
"below" us)	*"above" us)*

Now, let's examine a sample of each type in operation:

An unconscious instinctive reaction to an attacking poisonous snake would be for you to flee at unusual speed, not likely in your everyday life. Without conscious thought passing through your mind, you might leap high into the air and literally "fly" toward safer space, where the snake could not reach you. Or you might know stories where a parent used superhuman strength to perform a physically "impossible" feat when a child was in a life-or-death situation. Another example of an instinctual reaction would be a fixed biological craving (alcoholism).

In a similar way, if we are threatened psychologically, we can become unconsciously driven by an archetypal reaction. You might be under the influence, for example, of "a Mother complex"—meaning you've never resolved certain issues with your mother, who never let you be yourself. And even though you may now be over forty years old, when the phone rings and your mother's voice is heard at the other end of the line, you react viscerally. Unconsciously then, if you are under the influence of a "Negative Mother" archetype, you react to all female authority figures in the same manner you do to your mother when a vague reminder presents itself in your life.

You might be in your office, minding your own business, and your female boss walks in, giving you an order in a rather abrupt manner. Instead of simply taking it in stride, or telling her no politely, you overreact viscerally and emotionally, perhaps behaving childishly. Your psyche was threatened by being overtaken again by "Mother." And it happened before you had time to think! Your response was automatic and did not pass through your logical mind first. Later, of course, you are probably embarrassed.

Voluntary motivation happens in the mid-range, not in the extremes. We know, however, that we all sometimes act out, through extreme instinctive reactions or psychological responses we do not understand; they seem to just "happen" when the right stimulus comes along. Archetypes cause us to react in our psychological life when the psyche is in urgent need of something. They are bridges between the unknown of our unconscious and the known of our conscious life.

Becoming fully conscious is the work of psychospiritual integration; therefore, both our physical instincts and psychic archetypes must be taken into account for our full embodiment of Spirit. This is where all our "complexes" and "archetypal identifications" come into play. Therefore, we must find ways to access the unconscious mind. Jung believed the archetypes are seeking evolutionary growth through us, as we are through them, and that they deserve our most vigilant respect while this great doorway is open between the human and superhuman kingdoms.

As egos we are spirits in human form; the archetypes are the forms of spirit. Archetypes are our mirrored reflection in a higher dimension, as we are theirs in this earthly one.

Any time we run to the edge of what we know and reach the "chasm of the unknown," an archetype that is the *nucleus* of what we're needing next will constellate and bring us its qualities. We are victims of our unconscious mind until we make its contents conscious. Symbol or symptom; it's up to us. This is when the artistry of the Self becomes the most inventive: those magical synchronistic experiences will be evident all around you. Symbols from your inner psychic life of dreams and secret longings will show up in the outer world, signposts to show you you're on your path. At times like this, you are accessing Reality with a capital "R," which Jung called the *unus mundus*—a reuniting of the spiritual position, the Reality of a world where man can acquire some knowledge of his paradoxical wholeness. (1970, Vol. 14: para. 679) According to Jung:

Archetypes are complexes of human experience that come upon us like fate, and their effects are felt in our most personal life. (1968, Part I: 30)

—

THE TRANSCENDENT FUNCTION

The archetypes are the "magnet" that pulls us "up to the top of the triangle" anytime we're caught in a duality. This is their purpose, to keep luring us with their numinous charms until they draw us all the way into unification of whatever polarity we're working through. Their energetic pull on us serves a transcendent function. They force us to evolve. We can either go kicking and screaming by remaining unconscious of their hold on our psyches, or we can choose to get to know them and cooperate with their sacred purpose for our lives.

—

OUR PROBLEMS ARE NEVER "JUST PERSONAL"

Psychological complexes, which Freud and Jung both saw as our unconscious "unfinished business" are archetypal, too. Now, let's go more into detail concerning this troublesome aspect of our universality.

Most of humanity, when looked at through the eyes of wholeness, evidence for us a similarity in the human issues in which they get caught. It all begins to clear up when we view ourselves as one Soul. This helps us in two ways: (1) We stop feeling so alone when we realize how many other people in the world undergo nearly the same issues we do, and many have lived to tell the tale! It's always encouraging to know when we are feeling at our "bottom." And (2) We stop taking our own personal issues too seriously, feeling victimized by life or picked on by God. For this attitude truly is dysfunctional and gets us absolutely nowhere.

A complex is an example of an archetypal symptom that

takes on an important significance over some portion of our lives, distorting our here-and-now experiences with overlays of feelings, behaviors, and attitudes that do not fit our current situation. Though something in that situation will serve as a stimulus to stir the sleeping archetype and bring it into some form of activity. These triggers usually originate from dysfunctional parenting we had or painful, repressed childhood memories that never cleared from our subconscious.

Whenever we are operating under the influence of an archetype, we are for that time possessed by its qualities. This can be either a positive or a negative experience. For example, to come under the Child archetype when we are required to be adults can be quite disconcerting. Or to take on "Mother" or "Dad" when we'd hoped to be "Lover" is another discombobulating experience. Then, of course, if a *Puer Aeternis* (Eternal Child) finds a good Mother to take care of him, and she loves the idea, then this couple will learn a lot from each other. And this *is* a way to grow! We don't have to fall into a shame attack when we note that we are playing out one of the cosmic games. The key is to just be conscious of what we are doing; then we'll learn fast and keep moving along.

I've noticed, for instance, that when I make one of my dysfunctional projections conscious, I begin to see quite plainly that it's not the joy I'd hoped for, and it loses its flavor very quickly. I've often felt that this completes the fixation so I can get over it—to just allow myself to walk through something consciously, staying awake while acting it out. This can work in most situations, except, of course, something that is truly harming yourself or another person. No alcoholic, for instance, can *consciously* stay drunk, living in a stupor while discovering he's an addict! Nor can people prone to craving sex with children, stemming from unhealed incest issues themselves, use innocent children this way. Some patterns require complete abstinence and deep psychological work, for they cannot be handled in any other way.

Complexes, in the Freudian sense of the term, are archetypal fixations. To be conditioned by "a messiah complex," or "an inferiority complex," for instance, can have disastrous results. This caused Carl Jung to comment once: "You may think that you have complexes; but in reality, complexes have you!" You might say that archetypes, when worked with inwardly are *symbols* of aspects of prototypic people or processes you are working through. Within the inner life they are helpful in our ongoing analysis and transformation, but when acted out unconsciously in our lives, they become *symptoms* we must deal with.

So what is occurring when an archetype constellates and enters our lives?

- A field of consciousness is narrowed into focus through our concentrated intention.
- The power of the symbol we've invoked is highlighted.
- The pattern is enhanced.
- We image the archetype in our minds, while assigning it meaning.
- We begin resonating with its qualities.
- The invoked ideal activates instantly, beyond our ego mind's control.
- We purify our bodies, minds, and hearts to simulate the grand design.

LIVING IN THE "WORLD OF MEANING"
(WITHOUT GETTING ALTITUDE SICKNESS)

Should you decide to live your life symbolically, it will elevate you to a bird's-eye view of your ordinary life. This way of life is very fulfilling, for it puts you on the high road where your vision can expand beyond the limitations of the middle of your own picture, where the view is myopic. Events can be interpreted archetypally, where we can see the meaning and purpose in them. From this vantage point, everything in life can have sacred meaning.

Let's use the Shadow archetype to bring this point home. To think of your shadow as *only* a negative symptom, for instance, could make you feel bad about yourself. You might go from situation to situation in sackcloth and ashes, beating yourself up for being so bad. But limiting your view this way wouldn't let you recognize this archetype's sacred transformational function in your life. You would be missing the greater meaning behind all these events! You might even quit working on yourself, believing that you are a hopeless case, and you would fall into victimhood.

Or you might project your own problems onto someone else in your life, always pointing to the flaws in another. You could get so caught up in this that you wouldn't bother to look at this relationship pattern, asking yourself the *real* question: "How did I manage to let this experience become my reality? What is this kind of person even *doing* in my life?"

By recognizing, owning, and assimilating the meaning and sacred purpose of your ordeals and victories, you get clear. Through this kind of integrity, you'll gain a greater understanding of the "contraries" within yourself. Once you've made the pattern conscious, it won't have to bother you anymore; it will fade into irrelevancy for you and go bother someone else who is still living in denial.

In a World of Meaning the discrete events in your life tend to fall into clusters of meaning. It's a higher, more holistic way to live, and lots more fun! When we make this commitment to live symbolically, the light of the intuition activates and reveals to us the meaning and sacred purpose behind all our ways. We learn to read the keys from symbolism and mythology. Then, we can apply these as metaphors for our own personal lives and spiritual growth, and with open eyes watch them teach us. But here's a warning: To live in this high world in a healthy fashion, we must be willing to stay grounded in our ordinary world as well.

PICTURING THE "WORLD OF MEANING"

To live the symbolic life is to enter a higher reality. If you think of Absolute Reality as a circle, with the periphery being your outer life and the dot in the center being your whole Self, you can think of this World of Meaning as being midway between the two. Here you can gather all your apparently unrelated outer conditions into "meaningful clusters," making their sacred purpose visible.

To move into the World of Meaning, for instance, you might say of something: "Now, let's see the pattern here. What is this particular event in my life trying to show me?" And I bet if it's an important piece for you, it will have occurred to you many times over and over in your life.

For our purposes as people who are evolving toward wellness, living in this higher state of consciousness has many payoffs, as we can see. But it also has some pitfalls to avoid. So let me spell out a few:

1. We can never use "the high road" as a way to avoid a personal or interpersonal issue, or to rationalize a harmful or unconscious behavior in the ordinary world. This is spiritual bypass. As a social worker, I used to note that cities build large overpasses and elevated highways to block off the citizens' view of their impoverished areas. This way, a community can stay in denial about the problems that exist there.

2. You must never offer your own interpretation of higher meaning or purpose for someone else's experiences, unless you are invited to comment on such things. And even then, you must give these evaluations tentatively as being only *your* perception. This can be a useless and even harmful ego trip that can take you both off-track.

3. Be careful with whom you share your own high stories. Joseph Campbell had a favorite joke about this: He said you can tell the difference between a mystic and a psychotic because the mystic knows who *not* to talk to!

When people seem too preoccupied with telling me how enlightened they are, I know they are not. Having had an enlightenment *experience* and being fully enlightened are two different matters entirely. Anyone can have an enlightenment experience: This consciousness level exists in the Big Mind, and is available to all when the right circumstances prevail.

4. Though archetypes are us residing in a higher dimension, their nature is not physical; they have psychic nature only. They are not able to take physical form directly. As I warned earlier, it is a confusion of realities, and a very dangerous one, to ever think you've actually become the One and Only Archetype of something just because its energies may be constellating in your life. This is a form that psychosis can take, called in Jungian psychology "becoming identified with a central archetype." These are the jokes you hear about a dozen people showing up at a reincarnation seminar as *the* Jesus Christ, and all getting into a fight over who is the real one.

When you commit to the inner way, symbols start pouring into your life, along with those mystical synchronicities. Symbolic dreams and visions begin to occur regularly. Your ears prick up as you begin to hear others share from this level as well. Workshops and books on the subject begin to attract you. And your Higher Self now has another whole reality to bring into your ordinary awareness. You are living in a whole New World! And your life begins to glow with the light of personal meaning and sacred purpose. When we begin an ascension in consciousness, we merge with the archetypal reality's holistic patterns, where all the human Ideals for the new forms of life reside. Then, we open and receive their gifts. This is how the unconscious mind becomes conscious.

Chapter Eight

THE SHADOW AS DIVINE

*Danger arises when a man feels secure in his position.
Destruction threatens when a man seeks to perfect his
worldly estate. Confusion develops when a man has put
everything in order. Therefore, the superior man does
not forget danger in his security nor ruin when he is
well established, nor confusion when his affairs are in
order. In this way he gains personal freedom and is able
to protect the empire.*

—Confucius

ENANTIODROMIA: THE DIVINE ADJUSTER

Don't let the big word *enantiodromia* intimidate you. I can
hardly pronounce it myself. But I've included it here because it fascinates me to realize that the ancient Greeks
already knew of this great psychological law even before the
field of psychology was conceived. Jung identified this as
"the principle which governs all cycles of natural life, from
the smallest to the greatest" (1971: para. 708). Jung's recognition of the inevitability of enantiodromic change helped
him anticipate psychic movement (cf Samuels et al. 1986).

An emotionally laden fanaticism or one-sideness autonomously reverts to its other side when it has run to the end of its potential in one direction. *Enantiodromia* is a great psychological law at work, one that keeps us from becoming too one-sided. Instead, we are forced to know something from both sides. At some point, all extreme attitudes and feelings revert to their opposite to make the "unlived" side conscious. As we've seen, everything created has an opposite. Therefore, if we insist on only one side of anything at all, we'll be guaranteed a huge surprise one fateful day when the inner Self suddenly says, *Okay, time's up! You've learned all you need to know from this side of it.* The compensatory function of the psyche kicks in, and now everything will rapidly shift. We're forced to tumble all the way to the other side of our nature—the part that's being ignored, disowned, or denied. Our happiness turns into unhappiness, love shifts to hate. That perfect couple who never fight enter into a nasty divorce and a vicious custody battle. The fanatical preacher who raves at us about the sins of the flesh is caught in the arms of a prostitute. Exaggerated spirituality or "goodness" reverts to acting out basic instincts. We see evidence of this all the time.

When there are gaps in our conscious willingness to see and own any piece of ourselves, we can know for certain that the unconscious mind will compensate for this deficit and throw out an image in our psyche or an actual experience of it in our outer life so we'll deal with it. Jung called this process of something shifting to its opposite extreme by its Latin name: *enantiodromia.* This psychological principle was first outlined by Heraclitus and meant that eventually everything turns into its opposite.

The inherent workings of *enantiodromia* within our psyche will continually lead us to accessing and integrating our shadow. If you notice that someone is always good, always smiling, always anything, you will know that the shadow is probably hiding in the opposite that's never being expressed. This is a divine law of the psyche that has gone unnoticed and become a missing link upon many a spiritual path.

ACCEPTING YOUR SHADOW AS A CONSCIOUS COMPANION
(THE SHADOW AS "SYMBOL" OR "SYMPTOM")

The shadow is our passionate response to life, our heart's intensities borne from the suffering taken on so that we might enter fully into the human predicament. It is the first archetype we meet along our journey to wholeness, the first we make "real." It acts out so terribly, we simply have to notice. Jung believed that we meet the shadow by going through a narrow door—one that many wish to avoid entering. But it isn't possible to avoid this, for until the shadow is accessed, brought into the "light of day" and accepted with love and forgiveness, i.e., integrated, it runs—or perhaps ruins—our lives. It distorts our human interactions in ways that keep us unclear, victims of our excesses and addictions.

According to Jungian Jolande Jacobi, in psychic *inner* reality the archetypal Shadow is a *symbol* for an aspect of the self (1959). When we cannot find a way to work with our shadow through our dreams or in other ways, it becomes a *symptom* in our *outer* world.

Jungian therapist and author Jeremiah Abrams says our personal shadow came into play when we were about two years old. When as little children we were not allowed to be ourselves, our egos were not able to make conscious and integrate certain parts of us. As a survival mechanism during our developmental years, certain aspects of our nature had to be repressed, hidden away through denial. And there they remain in our subconscious to "cook." Psychic energy has no place to go when repressed; like a pressure cooker it builds, causing tension and stress—even physical disease (Abrams 1990).

Until it is made conscious, the shadow causes us to create emotional explosions and catastrophe or to explode in emotionalism. It stands there at the threshold of our unconscious mind, reflecting back to us our blind side. We must learn to embrace the shadow without trying to win it over. It is our teacher. Often we aren't even able to hear the more kindly offerings from our friends, so to command our attention the shadow must pop out and remind us that it exists from time to time.

The shadow is emotional in nature, not a "thing" or a certain "person" we can ever know concretely. It is often made up of our aggressive or sexual urges and promptings from the extremes, or some other "untamed" aspect of our human/animal nature. Since our rage and sexual desire are two aspects of human nature we have the hardest time integrating and respect the least, they are often the aspects of us that operate in shadowy ways.

According to Jungian Marie-Louise von Franz, the shadow takes the form of laziness, greed, envy, jealousy, the desire for prestige, aggressions, and similar "tormenting spirits" (1980: 123). When we ignore our shadow, it is like opening a door and allowing negative powers such as wrath, hatred, envy, lechery, or faintheartedness to step in. In ancient times, these were known as demons or bad spirits (von Franz, 1980: 116).

When we try to deny the shadow it multiplies. When we choose to integrate it instead, we gain stability and expansion of consciousness, losing our one-sided self-righteousness and becoming flexible instead of defensive and rigid. If your shadow seems to you to be fairly hard to accept, or you're having trouble finding it at all, you may want to ask for the help of a good therapist who is as at home in the shadow's domain as in the light, acquainted with the wilderness experience we humans must travel through if we are to realize our full potential. Jung writes:

> Everyone carries a shadow, and the less it is embodied in the individual's conscious life, the blacker and denser it is. At all counts, it forms an unconscious snag, thwarting our most well-meant intentions.

Embracing Our "Sparring Partner": The Personal Shadow

If you're brave enough to undergo the task alone, knowing you have a great deal of ego strength, you can ask your shadow to show itself to you through inner work, using imagery or other methods that access your unconscious mind. You can go within and talk with your shadow in the silence of your mind anytime it constellates and begins to bother you. Or you can keep a "shadow journal" and write letters to it, letting it respond to you. Tell it you will accept it, no matter what. And that you will hold it in your heart.

Here is one guided imagery experience that will enable you to access your shadow more concretely. You may have a surprise in store if you think you already know who it is or what it looks like. Most people are quite surprised at who is there. Your shadow is part of your emotional life and defies analysis. You can't know your shadow intellectually; it can only be known through experience.

You can put this guided imagery on tape, if you wish, and play it back. Or you could have a friend guide you through it. Either way, be sure to use enough pauses to give your psyche a chance to do the imagery. (The dots represent brief pauses.) You can also use evocative music (without words) in the background for this experience. Music activates the emotions and makes the process more of a sacred ritual, and hence, more powerful. Guided imagery is effective when you allow time for it to activate in your mind. Be sure that you accept whatever images spontaneously appear, without struggling to change them in any way. The more spontaneous, the better.

If some image should frighten you, instead of running from it, command the scary image to take off its mask and show you who it really is! Be firm. You are the one in control.

A GUIDED IMAGERY:
MAKING YOUR SHADOW'S ACQUAINTANCE

Close your eyes, and take a little time to relax. Feel your body settling down, and open your mind so you can use your active imagination for a while. Take a little time to do this before you begin.

Then, using your imagination...see yourself sitting in a room, looking at a trap door in the corner across from you.... You know that if you open that door, your shadow will come out, for it lives down in the basement of your house.

As you look at the closed trap door, something underneath it begins to stir, and you know your shadow is there. You get up...walk toward the door (notice how you are feeling) ...taking a lit candle in your hand, and putting on a violet cape (to protect you if you need it)...open the door...and wait. Now, accept what comes out. (Take a long pause while the music plays and the shadow reveals itself.)

Notice what happens now, as the two of you relate.... Note the quality of your relationship.... Ask it what it needs from you...and tell it what you need from it if it is to be a part of your life.... Now, take some time to just be with your shadow, and see if the two of you can embrace.... Notice what happens as the two of you merge.... If you could not come together, notice what does happen, and make a contract to meet with it again at some later time.... See what it does or says....

Find a way to end your contact with your shadow for now.... And gradually, within your consciousness, everything turns into a fine gray mist, and the scene begins to fade.... Now, you are sitting on the couch again, in that same room, alone once more. With your eyes still closed, take a moment to reflect on what just occurred....

Now, come gradually back from this experience.... Feel yourself to be fully back in your body. You may want to move a few muscles, to come more fully back.... And when you feel ready, open your eyes and take some time to look around the room and ground yourself.

Once you are back, you may want to write down what happened. This is similar to dream work. If you do not write it down, draw a picture or otherwise externalize this experience, or it could fade into a sense of irrelevance. Now, just sit quietly for a while and reflect on what you learned from this experience.

———

THE SHADOW'S SACRED GIFT:
ENHANCING ALIVENESS

To live a transformative life and avoid the *enantiodromia* pendulum, one must find that place of tension right at the "zero-point" in the exact middle between opposites—and learn to live there, not needing to identify with either extreme, but in acceptance of both sides at once. For example, when you hear yourself beginning to sound as if you're taking an all-or-none stance, stop for a moment and listen to yourself. Then bring in a little balance: *Well, though I feel I am totally right about this, perhaps the other side does have a point. At least I can be patient and listen.* Then, relax a little and stop taking yourself so seriously. Otherwise, Life may start living you, and remove all that control you think you have!

Anytime you find yourself caught up in a negative condition, stop and ask yourself: *What would be this disastrous quality's positive counterpart? What would I need to counteract this tendency in me?* And let an image come of the "helper" you require. This will constellate the archetype that is hiding in your unconscious mind, trapped by your own denial and lack of recognition of its power.

For example, let's say you are furious because your boss said something that made you feel inept and unappreciated.

Your day has turned into a funk and you are sullen, have no appetite, and find that at every opportunity you are saying something sarcastic about your boss. Well, your boss has gone merrily on the way, so obviously, this is *your* problem! You're the one left stewing. So take some time now to remove yourself from your activities, sit down somewhere quiet, and go within.

Who is this sullen person you've become? Get an image. Once you see him, her, or it, take some time to commune with it. See what it needs; let it tell you. (This is done simply through a silent inner dialogue that takes very little time.) Now ask it to bring forth its mate in the inner life. And take some time to observe through your inner eye who comes upon the scene. If it was a pouty little child who had hurt feelings, for instance, perhaps its divine Partner is the Divine Child. Let your own imagination give these symbols to you. Once you get the positive, denied side of the polarity, invoke its qualities by allowing yourself to name them inwardly, and then take them on. This means that you return to your regular activities and begin acting as if you are this positive One.

Sometimes instead of ending with the positive side of the pole, there will be a spontaneous transformation right there within your psyche; the little hurt child and its Partner will become One Self. Either way will bring you some relief, and perhaps also a great new self-understanding.

Abraham Maslow called this "dichotomy transcending." We find the balance between work/play, selfish/unselfish, childlike/mature, and so on. And we see that we are both/and. In this way, we learn to "pull into shape" something new and higher that is on the periphery of emergence, while holding steady what we may still be in the midst of clearing.

My inner Self has had to teach me a great deal about extremes. For I can become a World Class Hysteric when I am acting out my shadow self! Southern women from my heritage taught me well. And this has caused me so much grief, I finally begged God to help me understand my passionate nature. My Beloved comforts me with this:

When polar opposites split to either side, they become visible and distinct. They do this so you can see your dilemma more clearly and deal with it directly.

I've discovered through inner work that this "splitting off" serves a psychic function. In Reality they are always two halves of the same invisible center. I must always ask myself: *What am I really seeking here? What is my highest aspiration?* then let an image come into my mind that represents the pattern for the whole matter. I discover which archetype has constellated, and I can wrap my mind around what I am dealing with.

THE SHADOW AS THE ADDICTED AND "NEEDY" SELF

Many a poor unassuming soul flounders upon the path of Self-realization. And quite often, it is through an addiction of some sort. And perhaps this is our plight: Without a philosophy that honors both our psychological and spiritual "parts," we spiritual beings in human form cannot find the sacred and essential healing we require. We're all in need of healing, not from just one or two uncomplicated symptoms, but from having gotten caught up in the throes of the multi-faceted, paradoxical, and alluring human condition!

Addiction can be viewed as untamed libido, the human shadow running out of control and not giving us true gifts of the truth of our denied side. We can never be whole when we are involved in blocking out one side of our nature through severe judgment, denial, and projection. The shadow is craving expression to be understood.

If one side of us gets starved out, we create a compulsion. This can lead to dysfunctional addictions and unnecessary attachments. Or sometimes the shadow can get even more forceful and carry us to obsession: extremes, fanaticism, one-sided bigotry, dogmatic convictions, compulsive overactivity.

Closer to our ordinary lives, let's see what the process of addiction does within our personal development: First, we begin doing something quite natural—enjoy a bottle of beer, fall in love, get excited about a project, invest in a new interest, buy expensive things, or maybe brag about ourselves. And at some point, we do this natural and enjoyable thing more and more often. Eventually we become obsessive about it. Now it consumes our thoughts and our time. We sacrifice other areas of our lives to maintain a steady flow, and at some point we have lost control. Our self-esteem, our hopes, visions, and dreams begin to die and so do we. And we hit bottom.

It is as though we'd been living within the tension of a rubber band stretched fully. And suddenly, from the place of greatest strain, the tension broke! What has happened? We've been left wide open, raw, and vulnerable—completely "seen." And herein lies the blessing: *There is nothing now between us and our root consciousness.* All our defenses are gone, and we are utterly finished as that one we were before. We've run our old identity as far as it could go. And from these depths, a new life begins.

You can sense the transcendent psychological function in operation within our psyches. Within the addict's frenetic search to find what would finally be enough lies the key to our transcendence. The psyche, as we've seen, will push us to any extreme to force us to become conscious. Becoming an addict, whether we lose our freedom to a chemical or to a behavior, is so painful that we have no other alternative but God.

Addiction serves as a transcendent function. It is the shadow's movement through our lives giving us the experience that searching outside of ourselves for something to fulfill us doesn't work, eventually leading us back to our Source. Addictions are the negative side of our desire nature and show us who we're *not.*

BEFRIENDING OUR CONTRADICTIONS
UNLEASHES OUR CREATIVITY

Trying to regulate some part of ourselves we see as "wicked," "immoral," or "wrong" can cause us great trouble leading to a barbaric backlash. As long as the denied side remains unacknowledged, and therefore unexpressed, it builds up a tension that becomes the explosive, shadowy emotions that stew around in a cauldron of repression, denial, self-hatred, and misunderstanding. And it's only the lack of recognition as a legitimate part of us that the shadow grew into such potent force. When we can learn to live within this tension, meaning we acknowledge the paradox of both sides having purpose, the drama of *enantiodromia* will not have to take us over.

Sometimes people try to simulate equilibrium, but they are, in reality, sleepwalking. Balancing the tension between opposites may *appear* as "being positive" or as a state of passive nonmovement. But balancing the tension of the opposites is not like that at all; it is a pleasurable state of tension that doesn't pull us into a one-sidedness. When we are in this state the conscious and unconscious minds meet one another in harmonious play. We notice that our inspiration comes more freely into a creative expression. The healthy, creative person uses this tension for nurturing one's talents. This transmutation of energy, from being blocked and denied to becoming openly expressed, is how our shadow heals and becomes the *active dynamism of passion* in our process of co-creation. Our passions and true calling merge.

For you to become consciously creative, you must learn to bear your inner contradictions. Consciousness flourishes through contrasts—by separating figure from ground. When you explicate something by your focus on it, you are making it conscious.

Learning to live from center creates the contrasting design. We can move any which way, however the energies of the moment sway us. We can flow this way and that in open-mindedness, not becoming rigid at any point. There is no longer anything to get rigid about! For we are no longer trying to prove anything. Like riding a rainbow, we allow whatever colors are pouring through to have their natural expression. We are just being ourselves, with total acceptance of what is, and never are we experts on one side of the equation! Once we become this self-accepting, we can learn to love and accept others. But not before! The degree of our healing will determine the degree of our loving nature.

We can enter into the dance of the opposites, or we can remain aloof and nonattached. From the center, we see that we don't really have to hook into everything that's going on around us. We can remain The Onlooker, and become more selective about when to play ourselves into life or when to remain uninvolved. Whatever we focus and give our passion to will become our reality. We want to conserve our precious energy for the Sacred Work and not waste time on melodrama. As conscious beings, we have free choice.

But when we don't get the point, the psyche sets up a different way to present the discrepancy. Our errors then, and obstacles along our path, become great gifts, if this is the only way we can learn. That is, if becoming conscious is our goal. Once something is made conscious, it settles back into the *pleroma* of oneness, but now we possess a deeper sense of self-reflection, which is very pleasing, apparently even for God.

Chapter Nine

THE MYTH OF PSYCHE AND EROS

The complexity and richness of the archetypal world engage the evolutionary depths of the human possibility, while the passion and liveliness of the human necessity engage the creativity and deepening of the gods. This dynamic underlies our relationship to the Beloved of the soul.

—Jean Houston, The Search for the Beloved

Once we've made our shadow's acquaintance and have begun to clear up some of our shadowy, undifferentiated confusions about love and God and life, we can begin to resolve the split between our masculine and feminine aspects, and win the great "battle of the sexes." This is the Grand Dualism behind all others that we must contend with and make conscious if we are to ever experience wholeness.

In Jungian psychology, we have heavenly sent "soul partners," the *anima* (a masculine-oriented person's ideal inner woman) and the *animus* (a feminine-oriented person's ideal inner male). They can be troublesome for us when they remain shadowy and unconscious, and true helpful servants when they are made conscious. Their sacred function is to teach us the difference between real and illusory Love, and to excite us with so much passion and inspiration, we keep moving toward Home.

The archetypes of Psyche and Eros are "bigger" than the anima/animus, residing closer to our Source. They perform a sacred work (a transcendent function) that only "a divine couple" can do. They represent the psychic function of inspiring us to merge back into the oneness behind the masculine/feminine duality; that is, once Psyche becomes completely awake and realizes she is divine. For the longest time now, she (our incarnated soul) has been trapped in the human condition, not at all suspecting that she's immortal and belongs to the divine world of the gods and goddesses. When this awareness dawns for any one human being in the concrete world of form, the great cycle of necessity ends for that one, and rounds and rounds of lessons for the realization of that soul's divinity cease. This is the birthing and ascension of the new consciousness.

Try not to confuse masculine and feminine principles with the subject of sex. This is not a gender issue: We, and all of nature, have within us both an assertive and a receptive drive. One moves outward to express; the other draws us inward to express. This has nothing to do with whether you are male or female, or your sexual preference. When two people come together in matter in attraction and love, a polarity causes the attraction, no matter how you are oriented or which type of body you live in. This may, in fact, explain some of the dynamics around why we choose the love partners we do.

As you read, notice when anything starts sounding "sexist." And then, go within and see if this is a burning issue for you for some reason. We all know, for certain, that there are some distinguishable differences in the functions of what we choose to call the feminine and the masculine. Perhaps using the Chinese *yin* for feminine and *yang* for masculine, as you read along, will help you avoid any *unnecessary* distraction.

Now we meet the divine couple that Carl Jung was fascinated with, the archetypal Psyche and Eros. Their archetypal Love Affair represents the psychic function that inspires us to merge into the oneness behind the masculine/feminine duality. The story of these Divine Lovers tells of the soul's journey into matter and back into the heaven worlds again. The story symbolizes the marriage of the heavenly world of light with the shadowy underworld, and the journey of human consciousness into a new state of being. This myth came into being around 500 or 600 B.C., during powerful destiny-moving times when the Buddha, Lao-Tse, Confucius, Pythagoras, and Zoroaster were alive. Other great romances, such as Sleeping Beauty or the tragic story of Romeo and Juliet are also examples of this myth.

In Greek, *psyche* means "butterfly." As we know, this creature is a symbol of the metamorphosis that takes place when a living form goes into a chrysalis state, later emerging as an entirely different being—one who can now fly. Among many other things, it teaches us that impossible things are indeed possible.

So now, here is the tale of Psyche and Eros, so you will know the mythological story of the soul's divine journey in the material world.

Psyche was born an alabaster goddess, lovely, perfect, and unsoiled by human hands. She lived on Mount Olympus (symbolic of the unmanifested collective conscious mind) in all her purity. She was adored by the gods for her beauty and loving nature, so much that the citizens of Greece began to hear of her, flocking to admire this great archetypal Beauty, surrounding her with continual admiration. Psyche became so enamored of all this attention that she forgot that she was immortal. She abandoned her goddess duties, believing herself to be one of the mortals.

Aphrodite, the aging Goddess of Love and Beauty, was enraged that Psyche was receiving so much attention. So Aphrodite enticed her son-lover, Eros, to harm Psyche by shooting her with an arrow of love so that she would fall for the god of the Underworld, Hades. Psyche was easy to tempt, however, since from birth she had been filled with the divine quality of "sacred hunger." She so longed to be a mortal and experience the pleasures of the senses, she was tempted by the Underworld, and its god, Hades (also known as the god of Death).

Hades wanted her as his bride and lured her into his clutches by tempting her to taste a delicious pomegranate. She was compelled to marry this god of the Underworld and go there as his wife, destined now to enter the world of *duality* and take on "the knowledge of good and evil."

Eros, hovering near Psyche during her funeral/wedding, was prepared to shoot her with the poison arrow so she would never fall out of love with Hades, her dark and dreadful husband, and would be condemned to live forever in the shadow world. When Eros saw her, however, he was stricken himself by her beauty, recognizing her as his own "other half." Apparently, this youthful Prince of Love had pricked his own finger with one of the "poison arrows of love," and Eros swept Psyche off her feet right in the midst of her wedding ceremony. Therefore, her condemnation to marry death underwent *enantiodromia* (a shift to the other side of the pole), removing her from her plight and taking her back to the paradise with him as her Divine Lover-Husband. Eros represents the ability to take earthly love to a state beyond that of perfection.

Psyche lived with Eros in their unmanifested paradise in a "no place" state, the night world of dreams. Every night Eros would visit her in her bedroom, and together they experienced bliss. They were deeply in love, at first in form, then later in soul. And they culminated as the perfect Lovers.

Eros warned Psyche never to look him in the face, as gods cannot be seen as their true identities. And he told her they must keep their love in the dreamworld, to protect it from becoming ordinary. This was fine with Psyche, who was completely fulfilled by her union with her Beloved.

Psyche's sisters and close friends, however, became extremely jealous of her newfound joy with Eros. And they began to instill doubt in Psyche's mind about who this Lover of the Night really was. They told her he was only a part of her imagination and was not real. If he was indeed a god, they warned, why did he have to be so secretive in his ways of meeting Psyche, only coming to her on the inner side of life, in the darkness of the dream state? Why didn't he come out into the light of "the real world"? They convinced her that this type of rapturous unmanifested love could never fulfill her.

One night, overcome with doubt and curiosity, Psyche waited until Eros was asleep. She lit a candle-stick so she could steal a secret glance at her Beloved. As she looked upon his form, she was struck by his perfection and beauty; indeed he was the God of Love and Inspiration. Unfortunately, just as she noticed this, a drop of hot candle wax fell upon Eros, awakening him. He was enraged. Now Psyche had ruined it all! He fled as quickly as he could, back into the unmanifested collective, feeling betrayed by his one and only Love.

Psyche mourned her lost love and became willing to undergo whatever tasks Aphrodite, the Goddess of Love and Beauty, gave her to perform in order to win back her Lover. Aphrodite assigned her four impossible tasks, resting assured that Psyche would fail. She was to sort a huge pile of seeds, putting each one in its proper place. She was so overwhelmed by this impossible chore, the gods sent her a team of ants to help her. And with their aid, the task was accomplished. She learned the secret of "going with" our nature in complete faith that we are guided by our deepest instincts, modeled for her by the colony of ants.

Next, she was to gather the fleece from a flock of sheep. Sheep are symbols for a docile, harmless nature, yet these sheep were paradoxically crazed. Somehow Psyche knew that if she stirred them, they would kill her. They had become a potent and dangerous masculine force that women fear. Again, Psyche despaired and ran to the river to drown herself. Here, she was given another divine intervention by some singing reeds. They told her the secret of overcoming the sheep (in the night while their power is lessened as they sleep). They taught her the feminine wisdom of learning the nature of duality, of working with the pairs of opposites, and the importance of timing so as not to get caught up in the negative side.

The third task was then assigned by the provoked Aphrodite. This was to discover "the Waters of Life" by getting clear on who Psyche was and what Life is really all about. Psyche was given a crystal goblet to fill with the waters that feed the earthly world. And to do so, she had to face the Dragon (all the ways we go against our truth). For this impossible task, Zeus himself, King of the Gods, took pity on Psyche and sent her an eagle who knew how to fly past all obstacles and gather the water in the glass. The eagle taught Psyche the powers of clarity, the right perspective, the courage that transcends fear, and decisiveness. (If you noticed, what was happening was that Psyche was integrating the feminine and masculine powers within herself. She let loose her luminous feminine instincts and learned to engage her masculine strength without being overcome by it.)

Aphrodite now became inspired by Psyche's perseverance, so she gave her one final trial to test her immortal nature. Psyche was to journey to the Underworld and get from Persephone, Queen of the Underworld, her jar of beauty cream. She was to return by the same route by which she had entered the Underworld and was commanded to not open the jar under any circumstances. Again Psyche was overwhelmed with despair and climbed a tower with the expressed purpose of hurling herself to her own death. But as the gods would have it, the tower itself became her "divine intervention" and taught her its ways of rising above the trapping conditions of earthly life.

Psyche was carefully instructed to avoid four

"hooks" that could carry her away from her purpose: a dead man who tried to drag her into his decaying process; people with good intentions who wished to help her but were in her way; a man who represented getting caught up in one side of a polarity (the test of dealing with ambiguity); and the old women who warned her that she could not overcome fate.

(In this fourth test, Psyche was honed to stay focused on her own inherent wisdom and true tasks and not be distracted by what appeared to be generosity. She had to learn to say no to the good intentions of others who try to intervene with their own needs. Psyche was learning the power of discrimination.)

As Psyche carried the jar of the goddess's beauty cream to Aphrodite, she was tempted to open it. And succumbing, she fell into the sleep of unconsciousness again. Her deepest desire was to be with her secret Lover once more in the night worlds. Now she was willing to give up her life in the world of the senses to return to the uncreated heaven world. She would let go of her need to be mortal and simply focus on her spiritual life. Aphrodite was so touched by Psyche's love for Eros, she called upon him to rescue Psyche from her fatal sleep. This is the symbol of the death and resurrection of Psyche (our incarnated soul).

The story ends with Eros becoming Psyche's savior and rescuing her. He needed to pick the exact right moment to do this, however, for there are pitfalls in being rescued prematurely from transformational tasks. We must not betray our godly side, nor our human side either—as each is learning from the other.

Eros and Psyche were united once more at Mount Olympus (within the collective unconscious mind), and

Psyche was now relegated to the heights of her true station in life: an immortal goddess. She and Eros were married once more, this time sacramentally. In the giant uncreated Collective, on the inner side of life, their Love can remain a Perfect Love, not contaminated by human intervention.

Psyche models for us the journey into the earthly world, the tireless search for the Inner Beloved (the archetypal Self) through the process of transformation, and return to the remembrance that we are divine. And together, Psyche and her Beloved have modeled for us the transformational quality in relationships "with high callings" that bring us our complementary opposites. Together, they bring us the possibility of merging the archetypal and the human dimension of consciousness. In Jean Houston's words:

> *a saving of the gods through their gaining a more humane experience and compassion, and a transformation and deepening of humanity, allowing the beauty of ordinary life to surpass anything that could be suspected at the beginning of the journey. (1989: 186)*

THE GIFTS WE GAIN FROM PSYCHE AND EROS

If we were to look at the "labors" and qualities we develop to be complete, we would see that they are the same as Psyche's tasks, in the archetypal story of the divine lovers, Psyche and Eros. When Aphrodite absolved Psyche of all her work in order to win Eros back, we learn of four powers: the power of trusting our instincts, or deepest nature (sensing);

the power and practice of paradox, or working with "the tension of the opposites" (the knowledge of duality) (feeling/valuing); the ability to discriminate between what takes us forward and what holds us back (thinking); and finally, the ability to bring what we've gained into the world we are to help mold and shape (intuition). In other words, we have learned to spiritualize matter and to materialize spirit, the culmination of our sacred journey.

Now, our masculine and feminine principles live side by side within our one body as one androgynous being. We do not relinquish the qualities of either masculine or the feminine; they exist as an antinomy, opposites that complete and compensate for one another. Our true Beloved and only real Partner is consciously abiding within our very own selves.

Psyche's four tasks track perfectly with the story of Eve in the Garden of Eden, who chose to "eat of the tree of the knowledge of good and evil," and with Carl Jung's four basic functions and personality types: the powers of sensing, feeling, thinking, and intuition. In the Eden story, we see the same four tasks put before the courageous soul who leaves heaven and "falls" into incarnation. This is how creation takes place:

⟵

THE GARDEN OF EDEN STORY:
THE STAGES OF ALL CREATION

1. Innocence. First, humans were living in a state of oneness, the bliss of innocence. No part of us separated off and judged any other part. We were not even self-reflective; we just *were.* This is the preconscious state that aligns with our instinctive nature. We live through *sensing* what we desire and allowing ourselves to experience whatever comes our way just naturally, completely accepting of whatever the experience is. Since there is no judgment, there is no duality, no right or wrong. Pain and pleasure are both just experiences. Nothing is thought about, analyzed, or expected to be any other way than it is. There are no inhibitions, there is no shame. We are all naked together, just reveling in a state of being.

2. Eating of the Tree of Knowledge of Good and Evil. The second stage arises as a possibility—through Eve's curiosity and desire to "eat of the tree of the knowledge of good and evil." Eve was born with hunger. She craves experience. She wants to consciously be involved in creation. She begins to feel attracted to some things while repelled by others. Her heart ignites in yearning for the pleasures of the senses. Yet she also endures the pain of being in a human body. She feels her way into life, becoming more and more involved. As she eats of the tree she learns the lessons of duality. By traveling into this world split into good and evil, she loses touch with her wholeness. And she learns from the inside, out. She encounters one dualism after another, right and wrong, up and down, sacred and profane. Masculine and feminine split apart. Disease and dysfunction become a reality. Wars begin.

3. Discrimination. As Eve takes this mortal life, she learns how to distinguish between what carries her forward and what sets her back, what direction to follow, what to repel or simply ignore. Through processes of evaluation and judgment, she needs to *think clearly* and take responsibility for her choices. She meets the tests of spiritual discrimination. In so doing, she must find her center; she must remember who she is and the spiritual powers that she has, while living within the tension between the opposites.

In other words, Eve's task while incarnated is to remember her divinity. She must "stay above the battles" while simultaneously taking them on. She must not let "the fire by friction" do her in while she learns "to be in the world and not of it." As June Singer writes in *A Gnostic Book of Hours:*

> *How much suffering must we endure before we can begin to know ourselves?...life requires of us that we submit to many kinds of experiences so that we may comprehend what we are made of. In order to gauge our strength, we must be tempered by fire. It is an easy thing to praise the gods when they shower us with blessings. But when we have lost everything, our virtue, our pride, even our sense of who we are, it is not so easy to cry for help.... Yet the very act of calling out to God leads us toward an awakening of consciousness.* (1990: 109)

4. Brings the light of her knowledge to the culture. Wisdom is gained from Eve's experiences. She has learned how to "play the game." Having experienced the facts of the material world, she understands now the pitfalls of denying one polarity while honoring the other. As One who split off from itself into Two and can now self-reflect, she has become conscious and wise. Dualism is overcome, seen as an illusion that is necessary for any creation to occur. And a Third and higher way is seen, which merges back into the One, but now containing the knowledge of both sides of any experience. Eve learns to ride the opposites like two wild horses going in different directions, instead of trying to be just one or the other. The *intuition* is now honed and active within the Self. Eve brings to her people the fruits of her wisdom gained from the lessons learned. And at the level of original Oneness, God has also become enriched with the substance of His creature's experience. The *intuition* that is born of self-reflection is now honed and active within the transpersonal Self.

—

PSYCHE'S BURIED TREASURE:
THE REMEMBRANCE THAT WE ARE DIVINE

When we focus our attention inwardly, the bigger part of our psyche that contains our patterns of wholeness becomes visible to our inner eye. Recognizing our Creator-God as "the God-within" puts God right inside us, and this gives our inner life immeasurable depth and breadth.

When Psyche (or Eve) can remember to rise above her conditions while simultaneously fully entering into them, she is "doing the work of the higher world." An archetypal pattern is activated here on Earth, producing a high state of emotional tension. This brings together the conscious and unconscious as one; psyche and matter have merged. There is no longer any space between our divine life and our life in the ordinary world. As psyche and matter are two aspects of the same reality, this means we have experienced wholeness. The outer/inner lives are perfectly matched, having arranged themselves into a meaningful and identical situation.

When we are in this unitary consciousness, we are inhabitants of the One Real World. Carl Jung called it the *unus mundus*, as I mentioned earlier. It is during these times that synchronistic events take place: inner symbols and story lines coincide with outer events. And we say, "My God! I just dreamed of this last evening!" Or, "Look at this miracle! Could it be chance, or does this have a special meaning?" Their similarity of meaning given them *by our observation* is the "third element" beyond the two simultaneous events. And we are, for that moment, living in the Real World as the archetypal transpersonal Self, beyond all appearances of duality.

This state of *unus mundi* is the New Earth! This is the state of Self-realization. Our recognition of it and willingness make it so.

Chapter Ten

THE INNER BELOVED

This yearning for union with the Beloved . . . is the profound longing which transcends the desire for romantic love, the nourishment of parental love, and all the multiple and marvelous varieties of human loving, that calls us to our Source.

—*Jean Houston,* The Search for the Beloved

We begin to personify the soul through the archetype of the Inner Beloved. This form of the God-force within your psyche will move you onto the inner Path and increase the pace of your awakening. When this Inner Beloved lights the fires of inspiration underneath your feet, you are possessed with the need for union. At first you are not aware of its Presence as your contrasexual Other Half, the inner side of you that remained subjective and has never taken earthly form. This "Twin Flame" is your sacred "Beloved of the Soul," the "twin angel" of the Gnostics; this is the unmanifested part of your nature continually propelling you toward union from the subjective side of your livingness.

In the movie *The Butcher's Wife*, this other half was aptly called a "split-apart," a graphic description of what we feel about this "other" who complements our incarnated self, or personality. This Being lives in the subjective realities and communes with us from within—not from the objective world, though we meet many another personality from time to time who reminds us of this "Other." Almost everyone is interested in finding their true mate, searching for some person who is truly a spiritual counterpart. But your Divine "Other" is alive and well inside your heart! And no one can ever take it away for it will never leave you. Such a loving Healer of our abandonment fears!

This unmanifested part of us merges with the Divine when we "two" feel as One Soul. Jean Houston has said that we find the central influence of the longing for The Beloved in widely differing religious cultures, from the Sufis' ecstatic union with the One, to the Osiris/Isis myth of Egypt, and even in the remotest regions of the world where the Bushmen of Kalahari perform their "dance of the great hunger." (Houston 1989: 123) This inner Affair of Love has been the metaphor for personal transformation and human consummation in both orthodox and Gnostic gospels. We will create an image, feeling, or movement of our Beloved based on our ideal lover and the quality of relationship for which we've always held the supreme yearning.

TWIN FLAMES ARE A PSYCHIC FACT!

Real "Twin Flames" are a fact within the psychic realms. We do have a "split-apart" who adores us and guides us from within. This true Beloved serves the psychological function of keeping us moving toward our goal, of keeping "the dream" alive. This Counterpart is the completion of your very own Soul, literally your "Other Half" on the un-created side of life, as Eros was for Psyche.

But Twin Flames are just this: a symbolic Pair who serve a psychospiritual evolutionary function. Remember, your Twin Flame is *you*; you are and always have been one androgynous being. And he or she can manifest through you only by your connecting with this Beloved from within, and bringing the balance this archetype provides into your concrete life.

THE *ANIMA* AND THE *ANIMUS*: WHEN THE IDEAL "OTHER" BECOMES A STUMBLING BLOCK

When your real Beloved begins to activate within your consciousness, you can know that you are being called to balance the masculine/feminine polarity within you. This is the final task we undergo on our journey to wholeness. But this divine union can take many lifetimes, many suspect! And since so much glamour and illusion creep into this par-ticular archetype, I should warn you that if you think you're almost completed with this one, you may be getting ahead of yourself. For this "initiation by fire" doesn't come about easily. Before this great dualism integrates, we'll have the famed anima and animus to deal with.

The archetypal Masculine side of your nature represents the part of you that is logical and orderly, the part that dis-criminates, differentiates, focuses, and defines. It is capable of providing you with assertion and power. In your symbolic life He will often be a warrior, great teacher, a great protec-tor, practical and strong, ruled by the mind.

Your archetypal Feminine side is more relational, inclusive, nurturing, more diffused, soft, and receptive. In your dream life She may come through as a beautiful maiden, a mermaid, a seductive nymph or spirit who magically entices the male into the darkness of the unconscious mind. She lures the male onto "the path." She is perfectly comfortable in the diffused, uncanny world of spirit. She is magical and spontaneous, ruled by the heart. He is intellectual and in charge; she is intuitive and inspired. (Again, we are speaking of Principles here, not gender.)

When polarized and still imbalanced, we will have one side that is obviously externalized and more extreme, while the other is buried in our psyche, yet undeveloped. The undeveloped side will come in through our dreams, longings, and fantasized lovers who represent the part we deny in ourselves. We'll often project our missing or "inferior" qualities onto someone in our life to "do" this part for us. This we do unconsciously. Remember, for the unconscious mind to project our qualities on someone, we must be in denial about something!

A "masculine-oriented" person, for instance, may choose a mate to be "feminine" and "spiritual" for them. This way, this person doesn't have to develop this side. Or it might be the other way around: A very "feminine" person will select an aggressive, dominant, logical thinker to be in partnership with, so as not to have to deal with this side of life much at all. These imbalances are what Jung called the projection of the anima (feminine) and animus (masculine) principles. And they can make our lives miserable if we're unconscious of this imbalance occurring in our lives.

But let me quickly say: The Beloved *does* manifest itself

outwardly from time to time in various personalities that we meet. Your inner Lover can come through any person— spontaneously—any time someone is truly portraying the qualities of this Ideal for you. You will feel the upliftment and exhilaration that matches your inner feelings of Love for your Beloved. There is that "look" on his face. That certain "feeling" just came over me. That gesture, that quality in the voice. For a brief moment, an ecstatic moment, I recall a certain "fragrance" from some far-off time when we were together as One Flame. An archetypal Love such as I am describing is "an inherited possibility" of a representation that is able to manifest in this world through us when we are clear of our shadow's hold on our personalities.

Most often, however, the other person does not even know this is occurring, for it isn't a consciously planned activity. In fact, if someone is speaking to you of such matters through the lens of romantic seduction, you can know for sure the ego has hold of this process! When these times of outer manifestation of your Beloved do occur, if you are strongly connected to your inner Self, you won't have to act out in this situation, which could lead to falling in love or "playing around" with someone unavailable or inappropriate, which can lead to much heartache. This, of course, is how we learn. Much glamour and illusion, and *karma*, can happen in this deluded "lover's game."

I've never met anyone who does not have these feelings of hunger for total union with a mate. The archetype of Eros is the primordial human energy that causes our instinctual and ideal forms of love to merge. Sometimes our feelings of love glow with fierce fires that are both sacred and dark at the same time. Our process of psychospiritual integration will not proceed gracefully until we recognize the paradox of God's "paired nature" and we accept this archetypal dilemma as fact. For this potent Love to have its right place in our lives, all our illusions concerning the "faces of Love" must be encountered. All the glamorous notions of how "Divine Love" works need to be cleansed from our emotional life. Otherwise, our Inner Beloved can't get through to us. The animus/anima can carry us away into dramas and fantasies. We'll project God-like images onto one another, but we'll find that there is no human being that can make Divine Love to us.

If our shadow is all mixed up in the passions of Divine Love, we can seek partners in life with whom we can work these things out. And this is very important: We must eventually find the Self behind it all. In the meantime, these illusions can cause us to run down many an unnecessary by-road. So again, symbol or symptom, it's up to us how attached we are to these seductions.

Following is just one from the thousands of examples of potent archetypal Love, the famed pronouncement from Goethe's *Faust:*

> *Spirit by attraction draws*
> *Elemental matter,*
> *Forges bonds no man can force*
> *And no angel shatter.*
> *Double natures single grown,*
> *Inward united,*
> *By Eternal Love alone*
> *Can it be divided.*

Yet with all this unfortunate melodrama connected to our ways of love, we must remember what we know of our sacred power of desire. It's what keeps driving us, more than anything else, toward the manifestation of our God-nature in this concrete world. Sacred hunger keeps us fired up to keep heading toward our completion.

Uniting with your Inner Beloved is the healing of needy, obsessive love. You no longer *depend* on an outer lover to satisfy your hunger for love. It takes a while for this great truth to dawn on us as an experiential fact. And once it does, we never again feel alone, no matter what our outer circumstances bring.

When the archetypal Beloved is constellated within our psyches, we undergo an alchemical process that spins us into a whole new Self, one who is perfectly balanced between the masculine and feminine poles. This is, in fact, the act of creation in full swing within your consciousness. Your Beloved will evolve as does your Ideal; he or she may be very abstract and difficult to recognize—coming from the deepest place within your psyche. As you notice your inner visions, fantasies, and dreams, you'll see the Beloved come closer to ordinary reality, becoming more human in its image. It is "coming into incarnation" through you. Or as Jung writes:

> In communing with himself he finds not deadly boredom and melancholy but an inner partner, more than that, a relationship that seems like the happiness of a secret love, or like a hidden springtime, when the green seed sprouts from the barren earth, holding out the promise of future harvests. (1963: para. 623)

HOLDING "THE DIVINE TENSION" BETWEEN
PERSONAL AND TRANSPERSONAL LOVE

AN EXERCISE IN
LETTING GO OF ATTACHMENT

To release your attachment to the personal life does not mean you become cold, aloof, and unfeeling. It means you release your neediness in relationship that holds you and your intimates prisoners of personal, egoistic expectation.

Anytime you are feeling attached and all caught up in a personal heartache, you can practice the following:

*Close your eyes and breathe in **all that you feel, plus the air you are taking in.** Now allow the breath to merge into all that you feel. This will inflate the feelings like a balloon, and if you will hold this stance for a while, you will note that the feelings are being diluted and dissipated. Try this now, and see....*

The attachment to the personal life can be felt strongly within the cavity of your chest. Here, within the heart, we connect with the emotions and thoughts that go with personal attachment. Otherwise, our love would not be concretely felt.

*For example, your lover is leaving you to travel a great distance for a long, long while, and you are feeling that awful dread and aching in your heart, as you sit there with her for your final visit, completely awake in your feelings and aware of the **fact** of this situation. In other words, you are "at home" in the IS-ness of your love. You are **in** your*

*body and fully present in the moment. Now, as you breathe
into the feelings in your chest, tears come. A deep, deep sadness and sense of loss flood you, for this is the human part.*

*Now as you sit there, you begin to see that you can
bear the pain, as others have before you. Who hasn't experienced this separation from a true love? You'll note, as
you sit here self-observing, that when you dwell on what
has been and on images of the past, you fall into the feelings of agonizing attachment...and are overtaken by a
swelling sensation of grief, a deep hurting in the heart. Just
feel it for a minute....*

*The grief is a combination of passionate longing for relief
and a sense of dread at what is occurring out here and
knowing the sacrifice you must walk through. You'll see that
when you dwell on the illusion of the personal love and
those images of the past, you will fall into the feelings of
sentimentality....*

*Yet there is never really any separation—only a shift in
the nature of the expression, from the outer expression to
the inner knowing and complete union that no one can ever
take away! You are being given a lesson in true and eternal
Love....*

Just absorb this understanding....

*You are being tested to see if you can hold steady within the
greater context, the big picture, while simultaneously
**remaining in your body...and in an open human
heart.** (Our tendency is to abdicate the task, shut down our
feelings, and opt out.) You're being asked to hold both the
human and divine at once—a divine tension—to live them
each, embody them, simultaneously.*

Yes, we are all having to die to "our little family's heritage" as being the ruling principle that guides our motivations, and our movements through time....

This picture of who you are—as daughter, son, mother, husband—is vital, as it is now a part of you, a part that sustains heart-feeling and true compassion for humanity. But it is not who you are!...

These are the roles that you've been playing....

Now, take some time to realize and remember all of this.

Through the "science of impression" that comes in through our intuition and spontaneity, we begin to one by one take on the qualities of our contrasexual nature, our hidden "split-apart." Compassion, inspiration, creative expression, spiritual stature or assuredness, composure, certain talents . . . whatever we've lacked, these magical inner workings begin to round out our nature. We can begin to make this transformation of our earthlife a possibility— by looking for these soul qualities as they emerge through ourselves and "anchoring" them here by recognizing them. We can highlight them with our observation and respect, but we cannot program these "happenings." Archetypal processes happen through us—beyond the control of our ego's domain. As *a priori* aspects of the Self, they are already programmed to activate, and they will come to us in the fullness of time. Thank God!

It is by merging with our Inner Beloved that our creativity ignites into a blazing fire of inspiration for the world. And our wholeness is the spiritual gift that we give back to the world for giving us life. This is our service, our only Calling, really. The story of Psyche and Eros and their great love affair is obviously our story too.

Chapter Eleven

INITIATION:
AN INNER "PATH OF RETURN"

As the aspirant progresses, he not only balances the pairs of opposites, but the secret of his brother's heart becomes revealed to him. He becomes an acknowledged force in the world, and is recognized as one who can be depended on to serve.

—Alice Bailey, Ponder on This

MAKING THE U-TURN AND HEADING HOME

We are all Psyche, of course, as we are Eros. The two model for us the yearning we have to be whole, to be in right relationship to ourselves, to others, and to God. The gifts gained from Psyche's efforts to win Eros back, and the stages of her quest through the underworlds and back again to the higher worlds, complete the task of psycho-spiritual integration. This yearning of the human for a higher state, and the craving of the soul to experience the earthly pleasures, is the primordial undertaking we're all meant to employ to find our way back to our Source. The spiritual quest, as Ram Dass has said, is "the only dance there is." What else could ever outdo finding ourselves as a matter of the highest importance?

So now, our spiritual aspirations to be whole and serve a higher calling starts bringing us, as awakened spiritual beings, into our bodies, hearts, and minds. We no longer feel isolated and alone as separate egos; our urges are now coming from deep within us, emanating from our Core. Till now, we were busily involving in the outer life, taking on humanity's conditions, so that we could know them "from the inside, out." This is the only way in which a higher consciousness can ever penetrate into a lower one—to literally become it, then lift it up through *being* a greater Life. When any one of us makes this shift, from involving in something to evolving out of it, we are disidentifying with the condition, letting it go, because it's been assimilated and is now a part of us. You experience this disidentification stage as losing interest in the subject. You can picture this process as a V-shaped journey: we involve down into it, hit bottom (meaning we've gained or given all we can and now *know* it). Then we slowly—and at first, uncertainly—begin our ascension "up and out." This is how our consciousness works. And everything I'm saying now is a matter of consciousness, which shapes the outer world. You might recall now with greater understanding J. Krishnamurti's famous quote: "Our problems are not in the world; they are in our consciousness."

This shift of focus, then, from involution to evolution means we've entered upon the mystical Path of Return.

So now the scenery changes, both with us and without, for we're entering into a higher, numinous world now revealed through the lens of its symbolic meaning and purpose for our lives and for the life of Humanity as one Soul.

The inner spiritual meaning and the outer events unfolding along the time line have become One World—Jung's *unus mundus*, or what we've referred to in this book as The World of Meaning, which is the archetypal dimension of consciousness. This state of Self-realization has been recognized since ancient times. *The Gospel of St. Thomas* says

> And Jesus said to them: When you make the two one, and when you make the inside like the outside, and the outside like the inside, and the above like the below, and when you make the male and the female one and the same...then will you enter the Kingdom.

For the longest time now, we've had to keep our inner lives a secret—feeling shy or inappropriate about speaking of such things. Humanity has been passing through the "days of the Kali Yuga" (in Hindu terms), a giant period of sleeping while moving further away from our Source, sinking more deeply into unconsciousness.

Now, as if by magic, like a rubber band being pulled all the way out to the max, we're about to pop back home again. After a long, intense ego-experience, we are going Home. And because we already are spiritual beings, we already know how to do this, though we still may need to wipe the sleep from our eyes. We'll gradually start becoming aware of our true identities right here in the midst of our ordinary routines. Once we start to awaken, we'll begin to move so rapidly, we'll hardly have time to catch our breath. The forces of evolution have activated within our consciousness, and there's no turning back. This is what is creating that "urgency" many of you are feeling today. But because we are living in a dimension that unfolds in time, this embodiment of Spirit happens in stages, known in the "mystery schools" throughout the world as the process of Initiation.

THE STAGES OF EMBODYING SPIRIT

Initiation comes from two Latin words: *in* (into) and *ire* (to go), meaning "to make a beginning." Initiations are entrances into fresh stages of life. We've evolved from animal to human; now we are moving from human to "super-human." We go from ignorance to knowledge to wisdom. Knowledge separates things into parts for analysis. Wisdom synthesizes and unites. Wisdom deals with the essence of things and not the things themselves; it considers the whole. As we learn to embody Spirit, the knowledge of what we've "suffered" here collects into the wisdom of experience.

Before, we were ruled by our ego nature. Now as we progress on a path of wisdom, we are gradually overtaken by the soul, or Higher Self, and we become ruled by aspects of our divine nature. When this happens, the soul seeks its "path of return," already carved into the psyche, a remembrance. This path of return is marked by "initiations." These are times of significant meaning and purpose, when the personal intersects with the divine along the timeline of your life. Synchronicities will begin to happen constantly—where something outer will manifest as a representative of some inner psychic experience you are in touch with. You will begin to see the Meaning of all that you encounter along your road, as though a new Guidance is directing you, a new force of gravity pulling you to the right places and people at just the right times.

As we embody Spirit, we learn to distinguish between false and true, real and unreal, and to separate essentials from nonessentials in life. Through our inner development, we enter into the Big Mind of the Buddhists, or the "Mind of God." This is knowledge of "the kingdom of God within," the immanent God. And we understand the universe as "the kingdom of the God without," the Transcendent God of theology, as well.

Initiation is the soul's way of advancement, the soul's way of going to "Earth school." Through higher and higher levels of consciousness, the soul makes its way, step by step, through the kingdoms of nature—the mineral, plant, and animal kingdoms we passed through long ago. Now, it's the human kingdom we're "grokking." We progress steadily toward coming closer to our Ideal Self, or the archetype of Humanity as one Soul, entering into new and wider dimensions of the Self and life, through the expansion of our consciousness. We are becoming more inclusive of the soul's dynamic forces of intelligent love and spiritual will. Because we've learned what it feels like to be human, we are becoming a Master of Wisdom and Compassion.

We'll assume our identities as higher beings, until at some point our horizon enlarges and we can see the All of creation; we can see and hear on all consciousness levels at once. This is *continuity of consciousness*—our experience of immortality. We live in an eternal Now, where past, present, and future are one life stream. Through a sequence of revelations we learn all we need, both personally and transpersonally, for furthering the plan for all humanity. Every stage provides us with expansion of consciousness and enlightenment experiences where we see our next right step. You may have already experienced some of them; you probably called them "peak experiences" or "moments of religious ecstasy." They are those numinous times when you know that God has winked and said, *Notice this; it's a sign.*

Choosing to enter upon the Path of Initiation is a personal matter with a universal application—an optional *accelerated* path. This is a road we consciously choose at some point along our way that forces us to excel rapidly. Although we are all evolving and no one is left behind, some of us are still caught up in a state of "victimhood" and are not yet consciously choosing our lives. Initiates are consciously choosing even to suffer sometimes for a higher good. (The original meaning of the word *suffer* is rooted in the Latin word *sub-ferre,* which means "to undergo.") Initiates are old souls, and know they must sacrifice certain things along the way if they are to continually make room for "the new." They are not so bothered by such a fact. There is a quote from a metaphysical text, which speaks to this point, that has always made me smile. It makes this process sound so awful, it's no wonder this is the road less traveled! As Alice Bailey writes in *Ponder on This*:

> *See therefore how the life of all aspirants...is a life of ceaseless suffering, of frequent clashing with the environing circumstances, of numerous friendships made and transferred.... Ideals are transcended, found to be only stations on the road to higher; visions are seen only to be replaced by others; dreams are dreamt only to be realized and discarded; friends are made, to be loved and left behind. (20)*

Not exactly a way of life that anyone would wish to take lightly!

Our Initiation leads us into the alchemical Heart where we are "washed clean" and the tension between all opposites (and the secrets of good and evil) are resolved. Through sacrificing our old, egoistic, and personalistic ways, we gradually learn to stand free from rigid opinions, fanaticism, and one-sided narrow-mindedness. Here we truly love ourselves and our fellow human sojourners for being just exactly who we are: hybrid creations made of both matter and spirit, of both ego and soul. We learn to accept realistically—and humbly, I might add—our all-too-human side in all its errors and fragmented ways. And we also learn to accept the other side of our nature, which is just as difficult for us to own: our divinity! And from this place of both/and rather than the old either/or, the Heart teaches us Her mysteries "from the inside out." At every stage of development from this point forward, our horizon broadens and expands to embrace all that is both created and uncreated. Earth and Heaven unite. The soul shines through its instrument, bringing us its gifts of truth, goodness, and beauty.

THE FIRST STAGE:
GROUNDING OUR PHYSICAL/INSTINCTUAL NATURE
(STANDING FIRMLY IN OUR TRUTH)

The first stage of our soul retrieval marks where we master our physical body and reclaim our instrument and servant, the ego. At this first level of awakening, we are preoccupied with *handling our primary body/ego's needs for*

175

survival in the concrete world. We become physically and sensually aware of our true bodily needs. We seek to correct any negative patterns we've taken on that harm our bodies or lower our energy. We are carriers of light; therefore, we must shine brightly. If our energy is low or misused, we begin to lose this light. As we undergo our tests, we'll become very sensitive to the things that are making us sick and sometimes we'll develop symptoms of disease. We'll start to release all habits, appetites, or addictions that are now in the way of our physical stamina and well-being. And our bodies will gradually become aligned with our Higher Self. Here, we are preoccupied with our identities as physical forms; *we still partly believe that we are only our bodies—*and rightly so, for this is just a beginning.

Through our experiences, we are given the tests and conditions that teach us to turn our insecurities and self-doubt into their positive counterparts. We are required to find the soul qualities that balance or cancel out all one-sidedness or places where we may have gotten stuck in dysfunction. If we are committed to the path, we must master self-doubt and develop a strong and focused *will to live*. In short, this is realigning with our original purpose.

> *Beginning with the earliest emancipation of an "I" from the great sea of unconsciousness, it becomes that part of the personality that is repressed for the sake of the developing child's ideals—ideals which are individualistically reinforced by family and culture. Essentially, what doesn't fit the ideals of the developing person's ego becomes shadow. (Abrams 1993)*

If you grew up with parents who were neglectful or abusive, you may have trouble with this stage of purification. Your shadow might be plagued with a constant urge to "take you out" through compulsive or addictive behavior. And it may be resistant to change from having to defend itself with such vigilance. Feelings of terror, fury, isolation, and despair might dominate your personality in its weaker moments when your needs are grossly unsatisfied, and your shadow may overtake your ego during these times of soul-forgetting and confusion.

Our imbalances at this point can make a shadow of such density that we feel it is "me against the world"—a paragon of separatism. We may have taken on personality quirks, fragilities, or neurotic disorders as a reaction to early experiences that damaged us. For instance, if we were always told to be responsible and act "grown-up," our shadow side became the one who acts childishly irresponsible. Or if we were abandoned, neglected, and ignored, our shadow filled with unacknowledged and unexpressed rage.

We all have imbalances at this basic level of our functioning. Survival issues crop up in our relationships from time to time and act out through our shadow when our defenses are down. As adults, we may unconsciously seek partners to live out our early patterns of victimization and abuse. Until we make these conscious, they will be acted out through us. As we awaken in our bodies, we begin to see ways that physical gratifications had become idols to us. Now we see the need for balance so physical cravings don't run our lives even though—God knows!—these cravings still pull at us quite often and force us to remain strong in our spiritual intent.

MASTERING THE URGE FOR TOO MUCH OR TOO LITTLE CONTROL

This center of human activity is our very life force, our dynamism. We will automatically fall back on this level of consciousness when our lives depend on it. Physically, we master the appetites. And psychologically, we'll be required to master the urge for control. To pass this test, we must learn to "go with the flow" and stop obsessively trying to control or avoiding control altogether in our lives. We learn balanced self-discipline and our authority comes from within.

The urge to control was designed by our Higher Self to teach us to stabilize, hold steady, or remain in right relationship with others, the Self, and our circumstances. We may have an overwhelming ego need to be right, smart, good, or on top. Our personalities may have little tolerance for criticism, even the constructive kind. Beneath this need to control is the fear of surprise, spontaneity, or change. This lack of trust in life came from early childhood wounds. And some who were physically or sexually abused learned to use food as a way to stay in control of what went in or out of our bodies. So our eating habits are trapped within the shadow.

Our lessons include learning to give and receive appropriately and finally realizing we won't always be in charge! And now we need to let go of demands we may be making for parentlike support from mates and friends. Or, on the opposite side, we may need to let go of the urge to be a parent figure in our relationships. These are all distortions of "right relationship."

These survival issues that exist at the foundation of our ego life are the hardest of all to heal, for they are experienced as matters of life and death! Learning to remain open and honest about your feelings and your plight if you've been damaged is an important aspect of healing from early wounds. For we must learn to trust if we want to heal our wounds and remain in this world to fulfill our purpose.

The Transmutation

Once we reach a stable balance over these appetites and basic psychological needs, and become willing to follow the Higher Self, we've made it through this phase. And we can let go of our obsessive focus on our bodies and our survival. Lessons at this level begin to abate. Voluntary sacrifice of what we are leaving behind is always a part of the path—we die to the old ways to make room for the new. Balance and moderation are the mark of someone at this point.

Now we have learned to invoke and use the sacred power of *spiritual discipline*, the positive grounding force that transmutes our shadowy urge to over-control or be irresponsible. We balance in the center of the polarities of excess and deprivation. From the center, we can respond to Spirit. Spiritual discipline is the act of facing the truth in every situation and aligning yourself with it. Discipline brings these incongruities into the right proportion.

You might want to stop and take time to quiet yourself, simply telling your inner Guide to send you the qualities of spiritual discipline in whatever individualized package you need. But be careful what you ask for, unless you are willing to pursue it.

The Revelation

I am part of a Bigger Plan. I am not alone, nor am I an isolated ego; I am part of a Greater Self that has a sacred and eternal purpose.

We see that we are involved in our own evolution and have "our part" to play. We can let go of fear and begin to reclaim our true identities. We let go of any of our old passive victim mentality and enter into life with a commitment to be fully involved. We learn from the inside out how to take care of ourselves and to use the power of invocation to manifest Spirit. We see that we live in what appears to be two worlds at once, experiencing an outer and an inner life. But now that we are returning to wholeness, we sense that the two are one life.

The Spiritual Gift

When we master this ground level of our nature as spiritual beings in human form, we attain the *authenticity of being Our true Selves*, or the spirit of *Truth*. A part of the ego has placed itself in service to a higher order and is no longer focused only on personal gratification. Our attention is now free to pursue a higher goal; we have completed this stage of the spiritual quest.

Now our confidence that we are part of a greater plan manifests in our stature; people experience us as "having Presence." The channel to our Higher Self has opened, and our bodies are healthy and strong. Or, if we are living with some sort of physical handicap, it takes a back seat to the *elan vital* that is naturally flowing through, no matter what our physical condition might be.

—

THE SECOND INITIATION:
BALANCING OUR EMOTIONAL/RELATIONAL NATURE
(OUR GOODNESS IS MADE VISIBLE)

This second stage brings crisis in the control and balance of our emotional life, where the glamour of our moods and feelings overrides our deepest wisdom. We are reminded that we are not our feelings. At this stage of awakening, our emotions are purified. This is the state of consciousness where we will eventually feel what our soul is longing for; we yearn to serve in compassion and true love. Our emotional "body" is the source of the creative power that drives us to express ourselves as human beings, making life passionate and relational. Now we meet tests in life that teach us the difference between emotionalism and true feeling. We learn how our shadow can act out and carry us off-balance in our relationships with others. When our emotional "body" is not balanced, *we think we are our feelings* and we are driven by moods and overreactions. We might get "hooked" on others who make us feel especially good about ourselves or sexually alive.

Through the tempering of our desire nature, we develop a healthy *will to feel*: willingness to enter life with an open heart. When our feeling and relational life is flowing smoothly, we find an abundance of life force and an increase in physical stamina, along with a state of well-being or quiet bliss.

This stage concerns release of built-up energies that surge through us. This is the seat of worldly passions. This energy can be felt physically as the need to "push," much like that of the birthing processes. If this energy is tinged with sexual desire, it might feel like the need for orgasm. If we have not resolved all our emotional issues yet, our feelings can make us seem frantic, needy, or overly sensitive. Negative emotions like jealousy and rage can get a hold on us.

Emotional and relational imbalances are imprinted on us in early childhood, usually in families that had emotional or sexual dysfunction. Perhaps, as a child, you were not protected from adults' frustrations, outrages, hysterics, or sexual/romantic melodramas that you had no way of understanding. You may have become emotionally enmeshed with them, not knowing which feelings were yours or theirs. Your parents' feelings may have been explosive and dangerous, and you did not want to feel anything at all. If this is true, you may have "stuffed" most of your true feelings and distanced yourself.

Now your shadow may act out dramatically or passive-aggressively to gain attention. Through hysterics, outbursts of rage, or other ways of rebelling against significant others who do not meet your needs, you may be a powder keg of repressed emotions.

If, as you read, feelings are stirring up for you, aspects of your own early childhood may be coming up; you may be seeing some ways you've felt confused about your sexual and feeling nature. Please realize that if this is happening, it may be the beginning of a healing process, a recognition. A part of your shadow is uncovering itself so it can be seen, felt through, and healed. Once you make any of this content conscious, you'll feel a need to go on and release the old hurts and misunderstandings that are still living inside your body. You may want to seek a good friend or safe therapist to help you express these emerging issues. Remember, the shadow can only integrate by becoming known. So it may act out to get your attention. But you are always greater than any condition or negative experience to which you've been subjected. If you find yourself behaving as your shadow, try to stay light-hearted and as nonreactive as possible. You can talk with your shadow and "pat it on the cheek."

Struggling through life seeking "highs" or "looking for love in all the wrong places" is often painfully lonely. Constant rejection; lack of intimacy; competitiveness; and the need to be eternally youthful, sexy, and sensational— these are a breeding ground for chemical and other addictions. Problems with commitment, fidelity, integrity, trust, and intimacy are significant until the emotional nature is in balance. Not much security or love is possible until we make these imbalances conscious. This is the shadow's playground!

Because feeling states function dynamically, our emotional healing cannot simply be talked about; it must be felt through to be released. Shadow work is always experiential. In a setting where we feel safe and supported, painful feelings are emptied out, like squeezing toothpaste out of a tube. Processes such as breath work, psychodrama, emotional-release work, guided imagery, deep body work, music/movement therapy, and other methods can access and allow expression of pent-up feelings we're trying to ignore. Once we release them, we can see our life situations with a clarity that comes naturally out of living from the center.

Imbalanced emotional bodies like to stir things up. We might start battles when none need to be fought. The more dramatic and agonizing, the more gratifying, for at this stage of our development we thrive on the intensity of conflict. We love excessively, or not at all—a study in extremes.

MASTERING THE URGE FOR TOO MUCH PASSION, SEX, OR DRAMA

If we know we are currently going through this stage, we need to cease our search for happiness in other people and outer situations. Now is the time to focus on our own inner nature.

As we learn more about ourselves, we realize that attraction and desire are the roots of Love, our very nature. These feelings constantly ebb and flow from within us naturally. When we let ourselves act from our innate love nature, rather than running on fear of it (or of not getting enough of it), our natural talents and interests become our fascination. We can be involved in an eternal love affair—between ourselves and the Inner Beloved. Our desire will burn to create something. Our love can be expressed in a relationship, a career, some project or artistic expression, or in our life's work. Perhaps it will be an area of service that gratifies us. All of these elicit strong feelings of being "in love." They have a powerful healing effect on the psyche. Like the true artist, poet, or mystic, we can let this sacred creative energy express exuberantly through us. And believe me, if you invoke it, it will!

Now, here is a point I want to make at this juncture, which speaks of a very intense human issue—one we do not like to speak of aloud: We often confuse our sexual/relational nature with our urge for transcendence and expressing creativity. Our human passion center is the place in our consciousness where we learn to merge with others and all of life with enthusiasm and intensity. Devoid of these energies, we wouldn't have passionate interests or the ability to be creative, for we wouldn't be attracted to something enough to pursue it. In the archetypal/symbolic levels of reality, the urge toward incest is instinctual. It is the Self wanting to merge with its own nature. Therefore, if these images or desires ever manifest in your secret thoughts or dreams, you needn't feel that you are becoming ill or immoral; this imagery can be a source of deep healing *if* it remains in the process of psychic integration. But because these issues are so "loaded," they are best understood with the help of a therapist who is familiar with the workings of the unconscious mind. In the archetypal world, incest is only symbolic of something else. *In the personal/concrete level of reality, however, it is a serious and harmful violation, both emotionally and physically*, and has dire psychological consequences.

We all know that extreme passion and sexuality are the way we procreate. We may realize, though, that artists and inventors merge with something—a canvas, a piece of clay—to procreate offspring—a painting or a sculpture. To our unconscious mind, the instinct is the same.

The Transmutation

Our task is to invoke the quality of *Spiritual Discernment*. This soul quality keeps us from misusing our charisma and powers of attraction, or our dangerous "urge to merge." Call upon your Higher Self to bring forth this quality. The ability to discriminate will balance you by keeping you from indiscreet expression of your passion. For this stage of our transformation, meditation or quiet reflection is desirable. What *really* inspires or motivates you? Are these creative, healthy desires? Or are they your cravings, distorted from lack or pain in your life? This is practicing spiritual discrimination. Love and fascination are our lifeline—literally! But until we honor ourselves for being creative, turning our focus inward, we can waste our passion on irrelevant or self-defeating pursuits.

We can stop offering our "gifts of the heart" to the wrong people and projects. You'll discover your inner "observer self" will uncritically nudge you whenever you start slipping into a needy, dysfunctional pattern. Your Higher Self will train you to sit still with this feeling, and act it *in*, rather than acting it *out*. You can dialogue with it, journal, draw, or dance it—anything that will give it expression so you can safely contain this energy.

Until this level is mastered, the disciple at this stage of awakening views everything through a lens of romantic glamour and illusion, dreaming hazily of merging with someone or something in ecstatic union intense enough to wipe out the doubting self that hasn't reconnected with its Source. As we learn to look in another direction and seek a relationship with the Inner Beloved, our true "other half," we will heal from pain of our losses and disappointments.

We won't be able to balance our masculine and feminine energies until we do our shadow work and develop Spiritual Discernment. As long as the shadow is still lurking in the corners of our unconscious minds, we'll confuse every passing infatuation with our Inner Beloved.

This is a good place to stop and reflect on how Spiritual

Discernment might look in your life. What issues would you need to be more discerning about? Which areas of your life create the most difficult and painful tests? Go within for a while, and see what message you get from your Higher Self. By invoking Spiritual Discernment, you will learn the painful lessons that lead to your next full recognition.

The Revelation

No one or anything outside me can become a "tool" for personal exploitation of my deficiency needs. My "true Love" is within. The desire power of my soul is the search for my Self.

Until we make conscious our misuse of the powers of allurement and attraction—the magnetic and binding forces of Love—we will search for people and things as substitutes for the Inner Beloved.

The Spiritual Gift

When we learn to release our attachments, our feeling nature becomes benign and we become harmless to ourselves and others. We balance our energies of passion and allurement, charm and seduction, and become imbued with the quality of *Goodness* in this world: Our Love nature is grounded in wholeness and truth.

Goodness is harmlessness, but it is not perfection. Being in a state of Goodness does not mean you will never again act from misdirected passions, for we all will in times of stress. When we develop the quality of Goodness, we are more peaceful and refined, yet we are still fully involved emotionally as well. And we have developed a strong sense of "otherness," sensing with more care how our behavior is affecting others around us. Seeing the goodness in everyone and responding on that level is how we create heaven on Earth.

People who make it through this second stage and come out in one piece (for the trials are great since we *feel* them all!) have withstood the tests of the extremes. Now they can function in the world in the midst of uneasy conditions without losing poise or force. Goodness is *godliness*—high love! With a nonreactive emotional body, our minds can relax and turn toward matters of a higher order. We are developing free attention.

<hr>

THE THIRD STAGE:
CLEARING OUR MENTAL/INTELLECTUAL NATURE
(SEEING THROUGH THE EYES OF BEAUTY)

If we were uncontaminated or unharmed before we reached this point, we would have an intellect that draws reasonable conclusions, we would make choices based on wisdom and integrity, and we would have a solid, though not yet fixed, identity. Now that our emotional bodies are becoming nonreactive, we will think more clearly: We are able to *drop all mental patterns of illusion and seek a self-image that aligns with our ideals.* This stage awakens our personal morality: our values and ethics. This is an intellectual level of consciousness, where we develop our ideas, attitudes, and beliefs—our life stance. As we take on the trials and tests at this stage of our awakening, we believe we are what our thoughts have been about ourselves. Here we develop *the will to know the truth.*

The intellect becomes attached to stories about who we were *supposed* to be. We have always thought our true life was happening outside ourselves. We probably have struggled for a personal identity, possibly believing that emotional entanglements, comparisons, and competition were normal. Our ego formulated the face we showed to the world. Now, we reexamine those ideas and beliefs, for we are creating our true identity. At this stage, we are going to attract lessons about power, greed, success and failure, ego dominance, intellectualism, dogma, competition: in other words, the lessons of separatism and fragmentation.

People who are still damaged from early abuse or neglect sometimes have difficulty in thinking independently; they echo the opinions of parents, peers, or people whose opinions they perceive as more valuable. As children, they may not have been respected for their own feelings, ideas, or separate identities. They merge with the identities of their lovers or friends—sometimes relying on them entirely for emotional security, decisions, social life, or even to feel "okay." Writer Alice Miller believes many adults experienced "soul murder" as children, never being encouraged to think for themselves or to feel good about being who they are.

Sometimes families place unrelieved pressure on children to strive for symbols of success. Children grow up faking or lying to gain acceptance, bragging or flaunting success they may not truly feel they deserve: Their shadows become the facade that keeps them from finding a real Self.

If this has been your plight, you may feel that you're a phony. While preoccupied with the external world and its symbols of achievement, we can appear successful, responsible, and intelligent. However, we may not be fully grounded in knowing who we are! If we are still confused about our real identity when we come to this stage of becoming conscious, we are likely to go through a painful ego death. As our facade begins to crumble and is exposed, we may feel that we are *nothing* inside—that there is no real Self. This painful stage on the path is what mystics call "the dark night of the soul." It feels like your life has ended. And it has…until seeds of the new life begin to sprout within and around you. The way you've known yourself all along will change, and you will detach from the world of outer appearances. In *Unknown Man*, Yatri states:

> *The ego is a marvelous fiction…a false mirror…a novel written by ourselves about ourselves, and the very first step of the Quest is to disentangle ourselves from its seductions.*

Indeed, the ego *is* a fiction when operating independently of the Higher Self. But, paradoxically, without it we never would have survived the insults of our childhoods. The ego has served us well up to now as the instrument that relates us to a societal world. It finds a socially acceptable image and plays the roles we need from time to time. Jung called this self a *persona*, meaning "mask." The ego knows how to don the costumes appropriate for society at any given time and take on the human condition. At this stage of our awakening, we *consciously* play the game.

As we pass this through this "ordeal," the ego relinquishes control, and we surrender to the Heart. The mind shifts from illusion to truth: this is our *metanoia* experience, where all things are made as new. In Christ's life this was spoken of as the Transfiguration. All our values shift and our spiritual intuition awakens. Now, order and proficiency rule our lives. We begin to dream of the future and think realistically about how to meet our goals. This is the hallmark for the soul learning to live in human form. From now on, we will not fall into the illusions of materialism, attachment, and addiction.

MASTERING THE URGE TO MERGE INTO OUTER REALITY

This third stage is where we choose a new reality, having a new opportunity to decide how we will live from now on. We call on our Higher Power within to bring us the gift of *Spiritual Direction* or *Intentionality*.

The urge to merge is a function of the soul, but when the ego was damaged, our urge was misdirected. Until we surrender to a Higher Purpose and direct our devotional energy upward or inward, we throw this sacred quality away on people and things that bring only superficial rewards.

The Transmutation

Now we recognize this deep and powerful "urge to merge" as a mystical craving, a desire to become a part of the Creator and all of creation. We take on the attitude of the mystic. We yearn now to go inward to seek the subjective and numinous inner life. Now the ego settles down into right relationship with the Higher Self. We see that we had to take human identity and relearn ourselves "from the inside out." We were never intended to forget our spiritual identity.

The Revelation

**I know now that all truth lies within.
My outer life and all my projections are
reflected so I can "see" and correct
anything that is not built on love or truth.
All apparent opposites are really one,
joined by a higher guiding Principle or
sacred Cause that unifies them.**

The Spiritual Gift

Now we bring an integrated personality to the world.
The ego is in service to the Higher Self. Now the ego allows
the soul to shine through. If we fail this test of death and
rebirth, we will fall into our old habits and begin again with
many of the same old lessons we had before. Perhaps there
will be different faces or places, but our lessons and the
struggle will be the same.

This has been the soul's rite of passage from ego-domi-
nance to soul-dominance. We "die" and are reborn in truth.
As great sacred literature has promised, we are now "twice-
born," we are new once again. Says Stephan Hoeller:

*Into the life of every transforming person enters
the drama of death and rebirth in which one's
transpersonal destiny is met and accepted. (1992: 131)*

And we now possess the spiritual gift of Beauty, or Clear
Vision, pouring into our minds and senses, bringing us fresh
perspective. "Right proportion" is Beauty—pleasing to our
minds and senses. Beauty is "love made visible," awakening
our creativity. Arousing our imagination, this quality teaches

us to see all of life poetically and artistically. We see invisible promise and the sacred wholeness behind every fragmentation. We are living now where duality and unity intersect—in the "overlap between two dimensions." And we see that it is not through trying to be positive only that we dissolve all oppositions: All dualism dissolves in unconditional love for both sides of the Coin! Our love inspires us toward unification with our Source. We are Beauty; we are Love.

Emerson called Beauty "God's handwriting." We look out now at a world that appears in perfect order, even amid certain "imperfections." Balance and harmony have been healing our extremes of addiction and distortion. Now our lives take on higher meaning and purpose, for we see the divine order behind our individual story lines and dramas.

The shadow's life has become our passion; our *elan vital* is released for our true expression. We reclaim our whole selves.

Chapter Twelve

DETOURS AND ANTAGONISTS WE FACE ALONG THE PATH

All is God. But some things are more God than others.
—Ken Wilber

Now that you can see from the bird's-eye view your unfolding journey Home, let's heed the warnings of the pitfalls we must face and the inherent dangers along any path to Self-realization. This will enable us to heed the warning signs more readily and keep us moving forward with more confidence. In explicating these antithetical processes in advance, we disempower their influence on us. As with any shadow work, these inner demons only want to be recognized and honored for what they are. And remember: In spite of their onerary nature, they play an essential role in our process of growing whole.

THE OBSTACLES ARE WITHIN US

The blocks and detours we come across as we travel along our road are internal ones, and they will reappear again and again. But nothing outside of us can block us unless we give it that power. To overcome our obstacles, we invoke their positive counterparts.

DISCOURAGEMENT

When the lessons are hard, you may feel dismayed or discouraged, even despairing. But you don't have to let this stop you. This usually implies that you need help or support from others. You may want to take some time away from the outer world to meditate or go to a healing retreat or program based in love and support to gain inner strength.

Discouragement is healed through its sacred partner, encouragement. You can invoke it. And take responsibility for recognizing it when it comes. It will usually appear in your life from others' recognition of the ways you're doing fine. Validation and feedback are part of any sacred community. For we are a group soul.

PHYSICAL ILLNESS

The field of medicine has become expert in diagnostics and counteracting life-threatening symptoms to give the organism a chance to induce the more gentle and natural approaches of healing. It has created technology that can often save lives. But its weakness is in not guiding people in how to remain healthy and build inner strength. This is usually up to us. While honoring the medical world for its invaluable contribution to our well-being, a holistic approach to healing is often our own responsibility. We must always stay in charge of our own healing process, in concert with our inner Guide.

Working closely with the medical profession is a good

idea when symptoms are dangerous or too troublesome. Albeit, sometimes medical help can become overwhelming if you are given medications that stop your transformational process. If you can find doctors who use a "complementary medicine" approach, meaning they believe in both traditional and alternative methods of healing, you will find it easier to stay on your path.

To counteract physical ill health, it often helps to envision yourself as vitally healthy, as your whole Self. Practice daily seeing yourself this way, to the best of your ability.

EMOTIONAL "ROCKINESS"

Imbalance of your emotions during times of critical life changes and transformation sometimes cause you to feel that you are "losing it on the curve." And occasionally, you are validated for that fear by those in close proximity to your process, who suggest you go on Prozac or threaten to call a shrink! In other words, you can fall into a spiritual crisis quite easily while undergoing the storm and stress of deep transformational work. It's a good idea to stay around people who understand you, people who are also of "Initiate-consciousness."

Emotional imbalance is actually an essential part of the process, however. So we may as well accept this troublesome "symptom" as part of the journey Home. We heal imbalance by returning to our pent-up repression for ownership, discovery, and release. You'll recognize your emotional overreactions as those times when you've become too invested in an outcome of any sort. You will feel "clutched" and too intense. But we must feel it all through in order to heal it. So just stay conscious of your plight—no matter what it is. Serenity and bliss are the balancing factors for the temporary emotional imbalance. We can return to "center" anytime we feel we're getting too far off the track—take a long walk, or meditate. And humor always helps. As my youngest son will say to me: *"Come on, Mom, chill out!"*

At any rate, here's an exercise that will help.

An Exercise for Healing the Emotions

Take some time now to sit quietly someplace where you will not be disturbed. Gently inhale and exhale until you feel yourself calming down from your activities. (You may want to put on some soft, meditative music for this.) Gradually allow an image of yourself to emerge from within your mind. See yourself sitting in the middle of a Triangle as the point in the middle.... Feel this picture begin to present itself; feel the Triangle forming itself all around you. Notice how you feel sitting in the midst of this great structure...how you are sitting, what you look like. Be as specific as you can.

Now, very slowly, allow this Triangle to become filled with blue light, until you feel yourself encompassed in this warm and gentle light.... Bring it into your solar plexus, and on up and into your heart.

When your heart is full, imagine a point in the center of the sun where the "Heart of God" resides.... Allow yourself to merge with this Heart in the center of the sun.... Feel your mind, your heart, and your body become filled with light. And sit for a while in an attitude of calm reflection...in the center of the sun.

Now, gradually feel yourself sitting in your chair

again, in your room. Take some time to return fully to this reality. You may want to move around a little so you will come fully back into your body.

You may want to write some things down from this experience before you go about your daily activities once again.

FALSE GURUS AND EGO INFLATION

There are many charismatic people in the world, many claiming they are enlightened masters, or representatives from other dimensions. People may call themselves gurus, teachers, leaders, advanced beings, or extraterrestrials. Or create glamorous story lines that appeal to the young on the path; they often offer promises and alluring temptations for quick and easy ways to enlightenment. Some of them are truly capable of enchanting a hungry seeker! Many methods and techniques have been developed that *are* magical, but they do not always come from the Heart or from honorable motives.

"The lords of materialism" are all around us, and it's true that many false paths will appear at critical times such as these. They are our antithesis and are rightful players in any creative process, for they force us to use our God-given powers of courage and spiritual discrimination. Our powers of discrimination are essential for our protection and must be honed.

Following are some of the guidelines for you to use in deciding if a path is legitimate:

Signs That You May Have Taken a Wrong Turn

1. Listen to your inner voice, who can tell the difference between truth and untruth. You have a good

"b.s. detector" right inside your own consciousness, so honor it.

2. If the leader or group members claim that they are "the only way," and there is secrecy about much of their process that only the "inner group" is privy to, this exclusivity is a warning that something is amiss.

3. If the leader is too attached to being "enlightened" or speaks of him- or herself as "having arrived," it is a red flag.

4. If followers put down those who leave their chosen path, labeling them bad, wrong, sick, or deluded, you know something is off.

5. If the group or organization charges a lot of money that doesn't fit with the obvious outlay of expenses, or changes addresses often, or has trouble being validated by many people, or complains about the outer world as "evil," this is a sign of dualism and projection at work.

6. If the group claims a philosophy that doesn't fit in principle with most other recognized spiritual paths, then it may be violating the "law of parsimony." This means it has come up with someone's personalistic idea of spirituality or a leadership that is egoistic and doesn't fit with how "good works" come about and tend to validate one another.

7. If you are sworn to secrecy about the things you are learning from the group, or warned that you cannot seek knowledge or experience from outside this one path, watch out.

8. If, in the name of enlightenment, there are sexual, emotional, or physical abuses that in the ordinary

world would be considered abusive, harsh, or un-
loving, use your common sense. False gurus often
make claims that they are "above the law" when they
are really unhealed perpetrators, addicts, or megalo-
maniacs.

9. If you are being required to sacrifice your money sup-
ply for the sake of the group, yet you have no say
about how the money is used, you may be with a
false teacher who is needy for income, doesn't want
to do ordinary work in the world to support him- or
herself, and has no way of making a living except
through manipulating devotees.

10. If the leader or group members proclaim "unity consciousness" while calling you wrong or unenlight-
ened, they are the ones trapped in duality.

True spiritual paths are open, loving, and supportive of
your growth, no matter where you might decide to go or
what personal decisions you may make in your best interests. And the leaders will always answer your questions and
tell you what is going on. All spiritual paths may have sug-
gested disciplines, however, and you may be required to follow them for your own sake if you are truly a serious seeker.
But these instructions will have no feeling of coercion or
abuse, and won't dishonor your integrity.

We all have truth detectors in our hearts, so use yours
often. These intuitive nudges are the voice of your Soul.

Chapter Thirteen

THE TRANSPERSONAL SELF WALKS THE EARTH

The Self is "the Promise" within the midst of our existence. As the blueprint for the Ideal Human, the Self is both the ultimate source and divine completion of all our human experiences.

—J.S.

Being one who is agreeable, respectful of all creation, filled with delight and the joy of the sensual pleasures, the Self, who is the "Divine Outcome" of the marriage of Psyche and Eros, now walks the Earth and knows how to enjoy it fully. This is something our poor egos could never achieve on their own—which explains why many of us got so addicted or attached and miserable.

Now having bled off all "dross" (irrelevancies) and extracted the "golden nugget" (the real substance, or Truth) that was gained from our every experience, our bodies and hearts are impressed by the soul's emotions and the soul is embodied through our form. And now our minds are being impressed with our soul's way of thinking, which is through spontaneous revelations and symbols that bypass our analytical brains and just land in our awareness as direct knowing. As part ego and part soul, the Self is both personal and universal and serves as the mediator, interpreter, and transcriber through which these two modes of consciousness can communicate and learn to know and respect one another. We have a newly felt sense of acceptance of what is. And we are solid in our Self-confidence. We have Presence. For we've reclaimed our whole nature.

And this transaction—the acceptance of our whole nature—must become the goal of all treatment and healing programs. No other kind of personal work makes sense for people whose nature is both spirit and matter.

The Self Incarnate is a new state of consciousness for Humanity, and its true nature is that of a World Server. *This blossoming of our unique Identity is the final Activity on this physical plane of existence for our species*. And this "blossoming" is occurring now. And as said earlier, this is not a religious proposition; it is an evolutionary statement of fact.

THE "DIVINE INTERVENTION" WE'VE BEEN WAITING FOR

Divine intervention is an eruption in consciousness from our Bigger Story. These processes are what are forever renewing us. These images appear in our minds spontaneously beyond our ego's intellectual control. It is through these inner longings, glimmers, and visions of the holy or higher worlds that we continually see a bigger picture and a higher outcome. To follow these inner dreams is "following the mystery," also known as the Path of the Heart. This is spirituality-in-action. So you might say that our simplest definition of spirituality is this: *Our Spirituality is our life force— a continual movement toward wholeness.* It is our process of ongoing transformation—the movement toward greater heights or expansion.

When we say that something is moving or stirring us, we are actually being transformed. When we feel moved, an energy transfer is occurring. We are at that moment in resonance with our God-nature. In physicist John Hitchcock's words, we're in the process of "making a God-self in a God-world."

THE TRANSFORMED LIFE

Here are some of the payoffs to taking the inward journey back to the Source of our BE-coming and discovering that we are the Self.

1. We come now from our own vulnerability, having deepened into the chasm of the Heart and let out all our true and real feelings. Now we know better what we truly value as real and essential to our well-being. All nonessentials are gradually released. From the cleared-out heart a whole new dimension of consciousness peeks through, a state of consciousness we did not realize even existed: We see that the only way we can remain fresh and creative is through trusting our own experience.
2. The soul stands free—as a butterfly having risen from out of its chrysalis.

3. We are now valued for being ourselves. We are now living from an inner law—one that when touched enables us to leave and return with no fear of being abandoned or feeling lost.

4. The memory of how we change is now anchored within us. And we'll see that it tracks with our biological birth process—the first time, as this body, we underwent a transformation from one state of consciousness to another. We tend to repeat this pattern every time we're required to "take a leap into the unknown." Knowing this, we relax into however it is that we uniquely undergo a process of death and transcendental rebirth. Now we can do this consciously, instead of feeling a victim of the process.

5. We've birthed the gifted one that was hiding behind aspects of our shadow, having undergone the recognition, acceptance, and death/rebirth process that shifted our neurotic behavior into the fullness of its transmutation into its positive counterpart.

6. We are no longer trying to hold onto things that have outlived their usefulness, and we are now willing to live in the here and now.

7. We are perfectly comfortable allowing one experience to harmoniously flow into the next one, for living as the Self has that glorious feeling of being "at Home," no matter what is occurring in our outer world.

The goal of psychospiritual integration is to make us fully conscious, wise, discriminating, and able to be refined instruments for receiving the higher impressions of our soul. When we can manifest these qualities of the soul in our

daily lives with full intent, we are fulfilling our soul's purpose and the larger plan for Humanity. We are helping to
create a new culture in which our newly honed qualities
have become a part. This is how the healing of our individual psyches affects the whole, giving our little personal
lives and individual struggles a sense of sacred meaning and
connectedness.

THE NEW WORLD SERVER

Service is at-one-ment with the soul!
—*Alice Bailey,* Serving Humanity

**This "threshold work" creates a new kind
of philanthropist who is rising up from
within you. Some of you are connecting
with this archetypal World Server right
now.**

These new philanthropists are ordinary folk and sea-
soned travelers upon the path of direct experience, people
who have already hit bottom from their old ways—and survived! Some of you are connecting with this archetypal
World Server right now. In our work throughout the United
States and Canada, we meet seekers from all walks of life
who tell us they are feeling this Call and are anxious to find
their niche for they are discovering ways they want to serve
the greater whole. In other words, you are the ones who are
"going first." And you know only one thing in order to serve:
how to hold the rod of faith in the process, while birthing
the new life.

This new breed of Server works right in the overlap

between the two worlds, the one that is dying and the one taking form, which is the mystic's famed "cave of the heart." The human/spiritual heart is the bridge between the personal and impersonal life. We enter into this sacred chamber to redeem all aspects of ourselves, even our shadowy parts. It is from this Heart space, butt naked and raw, that we are made fresh and innocent once more through a process of psychospiritual integration. With gentle group support, we'll discover that all our experiences, even the hurtful ones, have served a sacred purpose for the unfolding life of Spirit. Our redemption lies in this recognition that it's all worked for the good of the whole.

The spiritual gift of having hit bottom is that you lived to tell the tale! By holding steady while the masses plummet into the natural chaos of rapid and dramatic change, we learn to serve by simply being ourselves, and modeling this authenticity for others and for our world that is starving for Truth. By our very beingness, we remind others that it's okay to die, knowing that living goes on beyond our fears, our disbelief, and even beyond our deepest humiliations. This sacred work of simply going through the process of becoming real brings us all into right relationship with one another and with our world. So, "doing your Being" is a spiritual path many will find themselves walking along today.

Because we are all connected in the deeper strata of Humanity's consciousness, we are all World Servers when we are just willing to work on ourselves and clear out our own consciousness. You never know when your particular clarity on an issue you've worked through becomes a beacon for another. Sometimes you are modeling something for someone else beyond your awareness. Or sometimes, just by being yourself, you are giving someone hope. Our task at the closing of this age is to have the courage to be ourselves.

Many of you have committed to this path in the invisible worlds and may be awakening to this fact today. Once you recognize this is your soul's intention, just to become yourself and be willing to share this beingness with others, you become a healer in the realm of the mind and emotions. Once you commit to this path and your intuition begins to flow into a more clarified remembrance, all who happen onto your path will be affected by your essential nature.

THE LAWS OF MANIFESTATION

Your changes will begin on the inner side of life, in the subjective world of your imagination. The first law of manifestation is "Thought is Creative"! Everything must always begin in the subjective world of somebody's mind. In other words, you will begin to experience any new creation first *as a possibility only*. Then, if you focus on it, imbuing it with the force of your desiring, the cosmic law of manifestation will take over the project and make your "thought-form" a realized fact. As Marilyn Ferguson, in her landmark book, *The Aquarian Conspiracy*, so wisely reminded us: *We can never have anything that we can't imagine.*

Our thoughts, when given the "oomph" of a lot of emotional desire and intention, are creative. And yes, this is a law of physics. Until we observe something and call it "real," for us, it does not exist. Then, once something becomes a possibility, the archetypal realm (which you now know a lot about) moves in and begins to shape our new possibility into a psychic fact, or form, and we begin to dream of it symbolically or metaphorically. This happens beyond the ego's control. And it happens most easily, unfortunately, when we are in crisis: The fires of transformation must burn high before a birthing can take place.

Then, it will follow the rules of manifestation and come on down into our outer reality as a fact in the concrete world. To manifest something, we

- Envision it
- See how it fits into the larger world
- Build a thought form of it in our mind's eye
- Put energy into it by desiring it intensely
- Separate out the parts of it that are too big or will not work
- Share our dream with others who will help us make it happen
- Do the practical work of building it or of being it

In our work, we are using the invocation, which comes from inner guidance. You may also find it effective:

Let Reality govern my every thought and Truth be the master of my life. For so it must be, and help me to do my part.

But you must be careful in saying this with feeling. For it works! It means that everything in your life that is based on illusion or a lie will be removed from you. And sometimes, not so gently! So be sure you mean it when you ask for Truth to govern your life.

From my work in our psychospiritual retreats with hundreds who are consciously carving pathways into the new, the following summation can serve as reminders for making the shift more smoothly—each to be enacted in your own natural style:

- Align your personal desires with what is good for the whole.
- Be willing to note your resistance, and then say, "I am willing," and surrender to whatever life brings you each moment of every day.
- Synthesize the seed-harvest from your past and carry with you that which you truly value, with a willingness to release all else.
- Challenge humanity's outmoded forms in whatever places you know are within your sphere of influence in the world.
- Balance the tension between conflicting ideals by continually reminding others of the good in all seemingly opposing views.
- Think creatively and image your ideal future and life's work, according to your own inspired dreams and messages from your inner guides and Teachers.
- Become a model of authentic living for a world that is starved for Truth.
- Be loving and light-hearted in all of your activities.

Today, because we are at the close of an Age, we're not just ending one little personal cycle; our whole worldview is shifting. This means that *all* our story lines and beliefs are currently up for a final evaluation by the unfolding Self. Our often one-sided ways of being that are all lopsided, in error, or incomplete are being challenged. Our obsessive

tendencies, our judgments, long-held attitudes, and preju-
dices...all are currently being placed upon the auction
block, ready to be evaluated for what truth they hold in the
greater scheme of our soul's evolution. Our very minds are
shape-shifting amid piles of new data concerning who we
are and what we've come here to do and be.

All our revered attachments and true achievements of
this ending cycle will stand revealed so we can choose and
thereby co-create a future that we desire devoid of any
shadowy aspects we don't wish to carry forward. Whatever
is exposed that is not to be carried forward into the
next cycle is called out so it can be named, integrated or dis-
identified with, and released. And this is the highest form
of "shadow work." It lays bare the sacred purpose of
the human shadow and the gift that our addictions and one-
sidedness bring.

If we are truly to heal from all the dysfunction and the
"sleep state" we've all been subjected to now for many an
age (for it has even contaminated our DNA!), we must recognize how healing actually happens, and then take responsibility for doing our part creating healing settings and treatment philosophies and therapies that reflect the truth of
our nature. The recognition of our intrinsic nature as spiritual and creative has not yet had the cultural or psychological impact that it must eventually have. Though many of us
intellectually agree, we've not awakened fully to the implications of this full identity of ours *as fact*.

Right now, our world, according to Jungian psychologist
Jeremiah Abrams, *implosion* is how the shadow is at work in
the collective at this time in our history. It is "cooking." We
no longer have anyone to scapegoat; there is nowhere to go

to keep our denial mechanism intact. So it's important now to bring a psychospiritual understanding to the world so we can integrate our emergent shadow.

Because these bigger patterns have propelled themselves from their latency state into a dynamic force down into the world, things feel exaggerated and a great deal harder to manage. Not only are our personal dramas arising for us to learn how to contain, but the big patterns of Humanity are acting out as well. Currently, we are dealing with the perpetrator/victim archetype, the battle of the sexes, and the greed and megalomania patterns; our massive collective shadow is exposed. We can see this manifested all over the television and newspaper columns around the world. It's coming out into the open so we can come out of our denial of these major conflicts that are ruining our chances of freedom and peaceful coexistence. And some of our favorite heros are sacrificial lambs for this process. We so make them perfect and glorify them in such an exaggerated fashion, *enantiodromia* sets in and they swing all the way over to their worst nature, raw and exposed, for all the world to see—and learn from.

We must always be willing to face any opposition we may not be dealing with, and to accept the whole subject of that which we are trying to work out. For instance, if I'm okay with being a victim, I have to accept my perpetrator nature as well. I can't point fingers and blame. For both sides of any conflict are one and the same karmic lesson. This ownership of the whole pattern will release the trapped life force stuck on either side, so we can relate to this issue from center and no longer have to play out either role.

Shadow work is currently the key to our continuity as human souls. For whatever we make conscious, we have power over its use; but whatever remains unconscious has the power to do us in. And as we uncover the Self who resides within us as the core of our being, we're in for a great surprise: We'll find that "coming clean" doesn't mean we have to relinquish our passionate nature. Quite the opposite: Uniting with the Self is the ultimate high, a reunion with our one True Beloved—and this time, in human form.

We, as Earth inhabitants, are rapidly hitting bottom. We can no longer live in denial of our shadow. Throughout history, at these "turning points" this less inner path of direct perception reveals itself to the few who take time to notice and blazes the trail that leads us Home.

Fortunately for us, from the beginning of time our Higher Power has sung a melody in the depths of our being. It's lyrics carry us to our subjective, numinous inner life, and our ego's dysfunctional ways of thinking will gradually fade into the background of our minds as we learn to access the Inner Beloved. The Self is rapidly coming into embodiment now, desiring only one thing: To manifest itself concretely through us as the completed Human.

Son of man, bathe yourself in the ocean of matter...for it is that ocean which will raise you up to God.
        —*Tielhard de Chardin,* Hymn of the Universe

EPILOGUE:
"FOLLOWING THE MYSTERY"

Behold I show you a mystery: We shall not all sleep; but we shall all be changed in a moment, in the twinkling of an eye, at the last trumpet.

For the trumpet shall sound, and the dead shall be raised incorruptible, and we shall be changed. For this corruptible must put on incorruption, and this mortal must put on immortality.

...then shall be brought to pass the saying that is written: ..."O Death, where is thy sting? O grave, where is thy victory?

—I Corinthians 15: 51-55

Our deepest hunger is to be immortal in this ordinary world. And since we are both human and divine, this deep insatiable yearning we have can be said even more simply: We just want to be ourselves. And our gnawing "discontent" will continue to heighten to an intolerable degree until we learn to creatively express the true gifts of our own unique and Spirit-filled nature—until we're able to finally relax into the continual act of just "doing our being."

The marriage of our ego and soul offers us the way. For Psyche materializes Spirit (Eros), and Eros spiritualizes matter. Our deepest urge is to walk in our God-nature, bringing heaven right here to Earth—or to wherever else we may wish to travel—perhaps even in all the worlds at once.

215

I asked myself the other night, *Just what is it that you want?* And as I began to write, in the rapid flow of my pen I saw that all of the things that poured out are *qualities of the soul*. Perhaps this is your truth as well, so here they are:

- I want to be forever creative
- And ageless, of course
- A lover—and to always be loved back, intensely
- Light-hearted and playfully intelligent, in *all* my affairs
- And of value to the world
- And filled to the brim with beauty and grace!
- I want to walk as my God-nature right here in this ordinary world

So—who are you? Where did you come from? And what *are* you doing here? Where is it that you might be headed? Holding these questions before our minds will keep us on our course. These are the *real* questions; all else pales into insignificance, when we're really honest with ourselves, whether in therapy, at church, in the midst of a love affair, or sitting in our bathtub pondering which chore has priority today. As we trek along, content to follow the ever-unfolding "Mystery of Creation," sitting right there beside us now will always be The Awakener, our Beloved, the Soul, who

> breaks into our daily routine to startle us with a challenge: We are to create in this world—[right now!]—the likeness of what we envisage the other world to be! (Singer 1990: 145)

So remember, when we finally discover the key to making our outer life compatible with our inner dream, our earthly nature as sacred in our eyes as is our heavenly one, and when our masculine and feminine natures learn just to relax and let each other be—*then*, the door to dualism will be forever closed, and you and I—and all of us—shall be free.

BIBLIOGRAPHY

Abrams, Jeremiah. 1993. "Tea with Our Demons." *i to i* April-June.

———, ed. 1990. *Reclaiming the Inner Child*. Los Angeles: J. P. Tarcher.

Bailey, Alice A. 1991. *Ponder on This: A Compilation*. Cooper Station, N.Y.: Lucis.

———. 1993. *Serving Humanity: A Compilation*. Cooper Station, N.Y.: Lucis.

Borysenko, Joan. 1990. *Guilt is the Teacher, Love is the Lesson*. New York: Warner Books.

———. 1993. *Fire in the Soul*. New York: Warner Books.

Campbell, Joseph. 1970. *The Hero with a Thousand Faces*, New York: World Publishing.

Capsansi, George. 1992. *The Eros of Repentance*. Newbury, Mass.: Praxis Institute.

Chwolsohn, Daniel. 1856. *Die Ssabier und der Ssabismus*. Vol. 2. Leningrad.

Desai, Yogi Amrit. *Working Miracles of Love*. Lennox, Mass.: Kripalu Publications, 1990.

Dossey, Larry. 1991. *Meaning and Medicine: A Doctor's Tales of Breakthrough and Healing*. New York: Bantam.

———. 1993. *Healing Words: The Power of Prayer and the Practice of Medicine*. San Francisco: HarperSanFrancisco.

Evola, Julius. 1983. *Eros and the Mysteries of Love: The Metaphysics of Sex*. Rochester, Vt.: Inner Traditions International.

Fox, Matthew. 1991. *The Coming of the Cosmic Christ*. San Francisco: HarperSanFrancisco.

———. 1991. *Creation Spirituality: Liberating Gifts for the Peoples of the Earth*. San Francisco: HarperSanFrancisco.

Ferguson, Marilyn. 1987. *The Aquarian Conspiracy: Personal and Social Transformation in Our Time*. rev. ed. Los Angeles: J.P. Tarcher.

Gass, Robert, and Judith Gass. Sacred chants and songs on audio-tape are available through Spring Hill Music, P.O. Box 800, Boulder, CO 80306.

Gawain, Shakti. 1994. *The Path of Transformation*. Springfield, Va.: Nataraj Publishers.

Gospel of St. Thomas [22], Nag Hammadi Library.

Grof, Christina. 1993. *The Thirst for Wholeness: Attachment, Addiction, and the Spiritual Path*. New York: HarperCollins.

Grof, Stanislav. 1988. *Adventures in Self-Discovery*. Albany, N.Y.: SUNY Press.

———. 1990. *The Holotropic Mind: The Three Levels of Consciousness and How They Shape Our Lives*. New York: HarperCollins.

Halifax, Joan. 1988. *Shaman*. New York: Thames Hudson.

———. 1991. *Shamanic Voices: A Survey of Visionary Narratives*. New York: Viking Penguin.

Hendricks, Gay, and Kathlyn Hendricks. 1990. *Conscious Loving: The Journey of Co-Commitment*. New York: Bantam.

———. 1991. *Radiance! Breathwork, Movement and Body-Centered Psychotherapy*. Oakland, Calif.: Wingbow Press.

Hitchcock, John. 1991. *The Web of the Universe: Jung, the New Physics and Human Spirituality*. Mahwah, N.J.: Paulist Press.

Hoeller, Stephan A. 1992. *Jung and the Lost Gospels*. Wheaton, Ill.: Theosophical Publishing House.

Houston, Jean. 1989. *The Search for the Beloved: Journeys in Mythology and Sacred Psychology*. Los Angeles: J. P. Tarcher.

———. 1992. *Godseed: The Journey of Christ*. Wheaton, Ill.: Theosophical Publishing House.

Hubbard, Barbara Marx. 1989. *The Hunger of Eve: A Woman's Odyssey Toward the Future*. Eastsound, Wash.: Sweet Forever Publishing.

———. 1993. *Revelation: Our Crisis is a Birth*. Greenbrae, Calif.: Foundation for Conscious Evolution.

Jacobi, Jolande. 1959. *Complex/Archetype/Symbol in the Psychology of C. J. Jung*. Translated by R. Manheim. Princeton, N.J.: Princeton University Press.

———. 1964. *The Way of Individuation*. New York: New American Library.

Johnson, Robert. A. 1986. *Inner Work*. San Francisco: HarperSan-Francisco.

———. 1991. *Owning Your Own Shadow*. San Francisco: HarperSanFrancisco.

Journal of Transpersonal Phychology I (Spring) 1969.

Jung, Carl G. 1968. *Collected Works* Vol. 9 (Part I), rev. ed. Edited by G. Adler et al. Translated by R. Hull. Princeton, N.J.: Princeton University.

———. 1968. *Collected Works* Vol. 9 (Part II), rev. ed. Edited by G. Adler et al. Translated by R. Hull. Princeton, N.J.: Princeton University.

———. 1970. *Collected Works* Vol. 10, rev. ed. Edited by G. Adler et al. Translated by R. Hull. Princeton, N.J.: Princeton University.

———. 1970. *Collected Works* Vol. 14, rev. ed. Edited by G. Adler et al. Translated by R. Hull. Princeton, N.J.: Princeton University.

———. 1971. *Collected Works* Vol. 6, rev. ed. Edited by G. Adler et al. Translated by H. Baynes and R. Hull. Princeton, N.J.: Princeton University.

———. 1973. *Jung Extracts: Answer to Job*. Princeton, N.J.: Princeton University.

Kavanaugh, James. 1993. *God Lives: From Religious Fear to Spiritual Freedom*. Highland Park, Ill.: Steven J. Nash Publishing.

Keen, Sam. 1991. *Fire in the Belly: On Being a Man*. New York: Bantam.

———. 1994. *Hymns to An Unknown God*. New York: Bantam.

Mayer, Michael. 1994. *Trials of the Heart*. Berkeley, Calif.: Celestial Arts.

Moore, Robert. 1990. *King, Warrior, Magician, Lover: Rediscovering the Archetypes of the Mature Masculine*. San Francisco: HarperSanFrancisco.

———. 1992. *The King Within: Accessing the King in the Male Psyche*. New York: Morrow.

Moore, Thomas. 1992. *Care of the Soul: A Guide for Cultivating Depth and Sacredness in Everyday Life*. New York: HarperCollins.

————. 1994. *Soul Mates*. New York: HarperCollins.

Roth, Gabrielle. Evocative/musical/movement audiotapes are available through Raven Records, P.O. Box 2034, Red Bank, NJ 07701.

Russell, Peter. *The Global Brain Video*. Penny Price Productions, (516) 431-2889.

————. 1992. *White Hole in Time: Our Future Evolution and the Meaning of Now*. New York: HarperCollins.

Samuels, Andrew, et al. 1986. *Critical Dictionary of Jungian Analysis*. New York: Routledge.

Satprem. 1968. *Sri Aurobindo: Or, the Adventure of Concsiousness*. Translated by Tehmi. New York: Harper & Row.

————. 1986. *On the Way to Supermanhood*. Paris: Instiut de Recherches Evolutives.

————. 1992. *Evolution 11*. Paris: Institut de Recherches Evolutives.

Satprem Staff. 1982. *The Mind of the Cells*. Translated by Francine Mahak and Luc Venet. Paris: Instiut de Recherches Evolutives.

Sheldrake, Rupert. 1991. *A New Science of Life*. Los Angeles: J. P. Tarcher.

Singer, June. 1972. *Boundaries of the Soul*. New York: Doubleday.

————. 1990. *A Gnostic Book of Hours*. San Francisco: HarperSanFrancisco.

Small, Jacquelyn. 1990. *Becoming Naturally Therapeutic*. New York: Bantam.

————. 1991. *Awakening in Time*. New York: Bantam.

————. 1994. *Transformers: The Artists of Self-Creation*. Marina del Rey, Calif.: DeVorss and Co.

Somé, Malidoma Patrice. 1994. *Of Water and the Spirit*. New York: G. P. Putnam's Sons.

Tielhard de Chardin, Pierre. 1965. *Hymn of the Universe*. Translated by Simon Bartholomew. London: Collins.

von Franz, Marie-Louise. 1972. *Creation Myths*. Dallas, Tex.: Spring Publications.

————. 1980. *Projection and Re-Collection in Jungian Psychology: Reflections of the Soul*. Translated by William H. Kennedy. LaSalle, Ill.: Open Court.

————. 1992. *Psyche and Matter*. Boston, Mass.: Shambhala.

Wolf, Fred Alan. 1989. *Taking the Quantum Leap*. New York: Harper & Row.

————. 1994. *The Dreaming Universe*. New York: Simon & Schuster.

Woodman, Marion. 1990. *The Ravaged Bridegroom*. Toronto: Inner City Books.

————. 1993. *Leaving My Father's House*. Boston, Mass.: Shambhala.

Yatri. 1988. *Unknown Man*. New York: Simon & Schuster.

Zukav, Gary. 1990. *The Seat of the Soul*. New York: Simon & Schuster.

Zweig, Connie, and Jeremiah Abrams, eds. 1991. *Meeting the Shadow: The Hidden Power of the Dark Side of Human Nature*. J. P. Tarcher.

INDEX

About the Author

Jacquelyn Small, MSSW, is an internationally known speaker and consultant on new-paradigm psychology and psychospiritual groupwork. She is the author of *Becoming Naturally Therapeutic, Awakening in Time,* and *Transformers: The Artists of Self-Creation.* As the founder of Euspychia, she directs a certification program in psychospiritual integration.

More titles of interest . . .

Finding Your Own Spiritual Path
An Everyday Guidebook
> *by Peg Thompson, Ph.D.*

Author Peg Thompson helps readers explore their own spiritual and religious histories; identify and heal old spiritual wounds; learn about prayer and meditation, ritual and worship, community and service; and begin to incorporate a spiritual practice into their daily lives. 217 pp.
Order No. 1509

Finding a Spiritual Community
Companions for the Journey
> *by Peg Thompson, Ph.D.*

Finding a Spiritual Community is a step-by-step resource for readers who are exploring their spiritual needs. These needs may include developing a relationship with the sacred, interacting with others on the journey, confronting new images of the divine, and adopting new approaches to prayer. 48 pp.
Order No. 5040

A Life of My Own
Meditations on Hope and Acceptance
> *by the author of Each Day a New Beginning*

A Life of My Own is the essential meditative guide for those looking for strength, serenity, and insight in their relationships with chemically dependent family members, coworkers, or friends. Includes reflections on having faith, confidentiality and anonymity, attitudes, control, and trust that can help readers live more balanced lives. 400 pp.
Order No. 1070

**For price and order information, or a free catalog,
please call our Telephone Representatives.**
HAZELDEN EDUCATIONAL MATERIALS

1-800-328-9000	**1-612-257-4010**	**1-612-257-1331**
(Toll Free, U.S., Canada	(Outside the U.S.	(FAX)
& the Virgin Islands)	& Canada)	

**Pleasant Valley Road • P.O. Box 176 •
Center City, MN 55012-0176**
